THE ITALIAN AMERICAN

FAMILY ALBUM

THE ITALIAN AMERICAN FAMILY ALBUM

DOROTHY AND THOMAS HOOBLER

Introduction by Governor Mario M. Cuomo

OXFORD UNIVERSITY PRESS • NEW YORK • OXFORD

Oxford University Press

Oxford   New York
Athens Auckland Bangkok Bogotá Buenos Aires Calcutta
Cape Town Chennai Dar es Salaam Delhi Florence Hong Kong
Istanbul Karachi Kuala Lumpur Madrid Melbourne Mexico City
Mumbai Nairobi Paris São Paulo Singapore Taipei
Tokyo Toronto Warsaw

and associated companies in
Berlin   Ibadan

Design: Sandy Kaufman
Layout: Greg Wozney
Adviser: George Pozzetta, Professor of History, University of Florida

Published by Oxford University Press, Inc.,
200 Madison Avenue, New York, New York 10016

Oxford is a registered trademark of Oxford University Press, Inc.

Library of Congress Cataloging-in-Publication Data

Hoobler, Dorothy.
     The Italian American family album / Dorothy and Thomas Hoobler;
     introduction by Governor Mario M. Cuomo
     p.   cm.   — (American family albums)
     Includes bibliographical references and index.
     1. Italian American families—Juvenile literature. 2. Italian Americans—History—Juvenile literature.
     [1. Italian Americans.]
     I. Hoobler, Thomas. II. Title. III. Series.
E184.I8H66   1994

973'.0451—dc20   93-46918
                                                     CIP
                                                     AC

ISBN 0-19-508126-9 (lib. ed.); ISBN 0-19-509124-8 (trade ed.); ISBN 0-19-512420-0 (pbk. ed.)

9 8 7 6 5

Printed in the United States of America
on acid-free paper

Cover: Lugi and Gaetana Marchese with their family in Milwaukee in 1911. Lugi Marchese arrived from St. Agatha, Sicily, in 1902 and brought his wife and four older children over two years later.

Frontispiece: The Fidanza family of Wilmington, Delaware.

Contents page: Nicola Vitone, an American of Italian descent in Salvington, Connecticut, in 1942.

CONTENTS

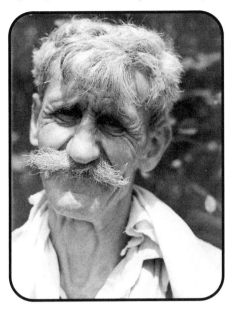

In 1982, Mario Cuomo became the first Italian American to be elected governor of New York State. He attended St. John's University on an athletic scholarship, graduating summa cum laude in 1953. After graduation from St. John's Law School, he practiced law in Brooklyn, representing community groups in their dealings with government. His work in resolving a dispute over the placement of a public housing project brought him public attention, and in 1975 Governor Hugh Carey appointed him New York's secretary of state. From 1978 to 1982, Cuomo served as Carey's lieutenant governor, winning election to the top state office when Carey retired.

Cuomo's elegant, thoughtful speeches—including the keynote address at the 1984 Democratic National Convention—have made him a nationally known political figure. Appropriately, he served as coeditor of Lincoln on Democracy, a collection of speeches by Abraham Lincoln, one of his oratorical forebears.

Governor Cuomo has been married since 1954 to the former Matilda Raffa. They have five children and three grandchildren.

Twelve-year old Mario with his mother, Immaculata Cuomo.

The Cuomo grocery store in the borough of Queens in New York City.

Three-year-old Mario with his parents and customers in the family store.

The governor, known for his eloquent and thought-provoking speeches, addresses a crowd in 1986.

Governor Mario Cuomo and his wife, Matilda, preside over the 1992 opening of the New York State Fair in Syracuse.

INTRODUCTION

by Governor Mario M. Cuomo

In the Provincia di Salerno just outside the Italian city of Naples, a laborer named Andrea Cuomo asked Immaculata Giordano to marry him. The young woman accepted under one condition: that the couple immigrate to the far-off land of her dreams—America. Andrea Cuomo agreed, and after marrying, the Cuomos made the long voyage to New York Harbor in the late 1920s. The young couple left the life, the language, the land, the family, and the friends they knew, arriving in Lady Liberty's shadow with no money, unable to speak English, and without any education. They were filled with both hope and apprehension.

All that my parents brought to their new home was their burning desire to climb out of poverty on the strength of their labor. They believed that hard work would bring them and their children better lives and help them achieve the American Dream.

At first, my father went to work in Jersey City, New Jersey, as a ditch-digger. After Momma and Poppa had three children, Poppa realized he needed to earn more to support his growing family. So he opened a small Italian American grocery store in South Jamaica, in the New York City borough of Queens.

By the time I was born in 1932, the store was open 24 hours a day, and it seemed as if Momma and Poppa were working there all the time. I can still see them waiting on customers and stocking shelves. And I can still smell and see and almost taste the food that brought in the customers: the provolone, the Genoa salami, the prosciutto, the fresh bread, the fruits and vegetables. Our store gave our neighbors a delicious taste of Italy in New York.

My parents lacked the education to help us much with our schoolwork. But they taught us every single day, just by being who they were, about the values of family, hard work, honesty, and caring about others. These were not just Italian values, or American ones, but universal values that everyone can embrace.

From my earliest days, I felt immersed in the culture and traditions of my parents' homeland. I grew up speaking Italian. I heard story after story from my parents and relatives about life in the Old Country.

Though not an immigrant myself, I saw the hardships Italian immigrants had to endure. I saw their struggle to make themselves understood in an alien language, their struggle to rise out of poverty, and their struggle to overcome the prejudices of people who felt superior because they or their ancestors had arrived earlier on this nation's shores.

As an Italian American, I grew up believing that America is the greatest country on earth, and thankful that I was born here. But at the same time, I have always been intensely proud that I am the son of Italian immigrants and that my Italian heritage helped make me the man I am.

The beauty of America is that I don't have to deny my past to affirm my present. No one does. We can love this nation like a parent and still embrace our ancestral home like cherished grandparents.

I like to tell the story of Andrea and Immaculata Cuomo because it tells us what America is about. Their story is the story not just of my parents, or of Italian immigrants at the beginning of this century, but of all immigrants. Our nation is renewed and strengthened by the infusion of new Americans from around the world.

Mario M. Cuomo

The Bianchi family in Varese, Italy, in 1885. Peter Pasqual Bianchi, at right, later immigrated to the United States.

CHAPTER ONE

THE OLD COUNTRY

The first Italian to reach the New World was, of course, Cristoforo Colombo, better known as Christopher Columbus. The son of a weaver in Genoa, Columbus went to sea at the age of 14, seeking his fortune beyond the shores of his native land—just as millions of other Italians would in later centuries.

Though Italian seafarers led the way from Europe to the New World, none of them sailed under an Italian flag. Columbus made his three epic journeys across the Atlantic in the service of Spain. So did Amerigo Vespucci, who was lucky enough to have the two new continents named for him. The ships of Giovanni Caboto (John Cabot), the first Italian to reach what is now the United States, belonged to the king of England. Giovanni da Verrazano, the first European to sail into New York Harbor, commanded a French expedition.

Similarly, the earliest Italian explorers to reach today's United States over land—Catholic missionaries such as Eusebio Chino and Marco de Nizza and intrepid fortune-seekers such as Enrico Tonti—planted the flags of Spain and France on what is today U.S. soil.

Though all these early explorers of the New World were Italians, there was no nation of Italy at the time they arrived—and there would not be one for another three centuries. Since the fall of the Roman Empire in the 5th century, the Italian peninsula had never had a single ruler. By the 15th century, such great northern cities as Venice, Milan, and Florence flourished as independent city-states. The pope ruled most of central Italy from his palace in Rome. And after 1504, the south of the peninsula, along with the island of Sicily, was a fiefdom, or the domain, of Spanish princes.

These political divisions led to cultural differences as well. Northern Italians spoke a different dialect from southerners. During the Renaissance, wealthy northern Italian merchants and bankers sponsored the artists and scholars who began a new age of culture in Europe. But in the south, people continued to live much as they had during the Middle Ages, eking out a living from the land through endless toil for feudal lords.

By the beginning of the 19th century, Italians were beginning to dream of a united, independent Italy. When Napoleon Bonaparte, born on the French island of Corsica, became emperor of France in 1804, he put his brother on the throne of a short-lived Kingdom of Italy.

After Napoleon's downfall, Italy was carved up again, but the dream of unity did not die. Among those who kept it alive was Giuseppe Mazzini, who founded an organization known as *Giovane Italia* (Young Italy). His aim was to rouse the spirit of nationalism throughout his country. Joined by Giuseppe Garibaldi, Mazzini organized revolts. When these failed, both Mazzini and Garibaldi were condemned to death and forced to flee.

Mazzini settled in London in 1837; from there he published newspapers and pamphlets to send his message of freedom back to Italians. He told them boldly, "Without a country, you are the bastards of humanity." In 1848, Mazzini was encouraged when revolts broke out in several places throughout Italy. He went to Milan, hoping that an Italian nation was about to be born.

When the pope fled Rome after angry mobs demonstrated in the streets, Garibaldi, who had also returned from exile, led a military force into the city. Mazzini joined him and the two men formed an independent republic. However, France soon sent an army that crushed the Roman republic and restored the pope to his throne. The other rebellions were also quelled, and once more Mazzini and Garibaldi were driven from their homeland.

From that point, the drive for Italian unification was led by Count Camille Cavour, chief minister of the king of Piedmont-Sardinia, Victor Emmanuel II. Cavour had started a newspaper called *Il Risorgimento* (The Revival) that was devoted to the cause of Italian independence. However, he dreamed not of a republic, but of a monarchy, with Victor Emmanuel as king. In 1858 Cavour made an alliance with France and called for Italian patriots to join Victor Emmanuel's army.

Austria, which controlled large parts of northern Italy, feared Piedmont's growing power. It declared war on Piedmont in 1859. But with the help of the French, the Piedmontese triumphed over the Austrians. This set off new revolts both within the Austrian domains in Italy and farther south in Sicily.

Garibaldi once more came to his country's aid. In May 1860 he led a gallant band of red-shirted volunteers in an invasion of Sicily. The peasant farmers, long oppressed by foreign rulers, rallied to Garibaldi's banner, and within a few months he controlled the island. Not content with this success, Garibaldi crossed to the mainland and began to march north.

Count Cavour, seeing a great opportunity, sent Sardinia's army into the papal states. His forces soon linked up with Garibaldi's, leaving only Rome under the pope's control. In March 1861, Victor Emmanuel accepted the crown of the Kingdom of Italy. Ten years later, the pope gave up all of Rome except for a small area called Vatican City. Rome became the capital of the new nation.

The success of the Risorgimento brought political unification, but the legacy of centuries of strife and

A street in Taormina, a village on the Italian island of Sicily, around 1900. After Italy's unification as a nation in 1861, most immigrants to the United States came from Sicily and the southern part of the Italian peninsula.

disunity still plagued Italy. As an Italian statesman said in 1870: "Although we have made Italy, we have yet to make Italians."

Particularly in Sicily and the area called the Mezzogiorno—the provinces south of Rome—people felt no enthusiasm for the new government. With their history of foreign rule, the struggling peasants of the Mezzogiorno had always given their first loyalty to *la famiglia*—their family. They seldom traveled far from their local towns or villages and saw no great benefit in exchanging one far-off ruler for another.

Indeed, the new Italian government seemed as bothersome as the old, foreign one. It levied high taxes, sent corrupt officials to govern, and demanded that the young men of the villages serve in its army.

Life was hard for the peasants of the south, many of whom possessed no land of their own. In the years after the Risorgimento, the Italian government sold off much of the vast landholdings of the Catholic Church, but the peasants could only afford to buy plots that were too small to be profitable. Within two decades, most of the Church lands were in the hands of the wealthy. Working for landowners, the peasants were little better off than they had been in feudal times.

A man who had left for the United States recalled his life in Sicily: "It was unbearable. My brother Luigi was six then and I was seven. Every morning we'd get up before sunrise and start walking about four or five miles to the farm of the *patrunu*—the boss. Many times we went without breakfast. For lunch we ate a piece of bread and plenty of water. If we were lucky, sometimes we would have a small piece of cheese or an onion. We worked in the hot sun until the late afternoon, then we had to drag ourselves home...so tired we could barely eat and fell asleep with all our clothes on....And life went on this way day in and day out."

Gerardo Belfiore brought to America this picture of his aunt and uncle with friends near Napoli, Italy.

A rapid increase in the population of Italy strained the ability of the nation to provide enough jobs and food for its people. The new government's program of introducing industry, primarily in the north, resulted in higher taxes.

In addition, diseases such as malaria and cholera ravaged the Mezzogiorno. Landowners often cut down forests for the timber and to clear the land for farming. This practice caused soil erosion, which created swamplands swarming with malarial mosquitoes. Natural disasters—droughts, earthquakes, volcanic eruptions, and phylloxera (an insect infestation that destroyed the vineyards)—added to what the people of the south called *La Miseria*.

In such conditions, it was hardly surprising that people sought to escape the only way they could, by emigrating. A traveler in southern Italy in the 19th century reported that the only decorations he saw in the one-room hovels of Sicilian peasants were "advertisements of steamship lines to the United States and South America." Immigration to the New World was the dream of people who found that a united Italy brought no improvement in their own lives.

In 1878, when a Italian government minister issued a decree urging the people not to leave their nation, a group of peasants sent him this reply:

"What do you mean by a nation, Mr. Minister? Is it the throng of the unhappy? Aye, then we are truly the nation....We plant and we reap wheat but never do we eat white bread. We cultivate the grape but we drink no wine. We raise animals for food but we eat no meat. We are clothed in rags.... And in spite of all this, you counsel us, Mr. Minister, not to abandon our country. But is that land, where one cannot live by toil, one's country?"

This map shows the borders of Italy between 1866 and 1919. Each district had its own traditions, reflecting the country's centuries-long division into separate states. San Marino is still an independent republic today.

Anton Fenoglio, who moved to Texas in the 19th century, kept this picture of his father in Ivrea, Italy.

LA VIA VECCHIA

When Anna Casatelli was 74, she recalled her life in Italy long before she came to the United States.

I was born in Italy on June 4, 1902. I lived in a small town near Naples with my mother, my father, and my sister and my two brothers. My father was an electrician; my mother was a housewife; and I helped in the house. I only went four years to school. One older brother was a tailor, and one was young and stayed home. One sister came to the United States, and one sister was at home. The one at home later became a nun in Rome.

For holidays the family got together to eat and drink and play and sing. The neighbors played instruments, and everybody sang together. Aunts, uncles, and cousins lived there; we saw them almost every day. Our town was small. We knew each other. Most of the people had small farms. Some sewed; some crocheted.... I started to crochet when I was eleven or twelve. I had girlfriends. We played outside. We went to church every Sunday night when they had Novena. In a little town, everybody goes to church.

I had a boyfriend. I don't know what, but something went wrong. His mother was a little against me. She didn't want her son to marry me. They had a lot of money, and he was in college. She wanted her son to marry one with a lot of money. I said to him, "You stay with your mother. I'm going to America."...

A friend of mine was going to Utica, New York. I had a cousin there, so I went to Utica. My mother and my father didn't want me to come here. My brother gave me the money to come.

Pascal D'Angelo was born in Samnium, the ancient district southeast of Rome, in 1894. Later, in the United States, he recalled the attic room where he and his family slept.

The garret was divided into two unequal parts. The largest in front where the roof descended very low was filled with firewood. In the small center part was the bed on which my mother, my father, my brother and I slept. A very narrow bed it was. Almost every night I fell, having my head continually decorated with swollen spots about the size of a full ripe cherry. The reason for these falls was my being laid asleep beneath my mother's and father's feet, because I was bigger than my brother and therefore could better guard myself. My brother was two years younger than I. He lay between them while they slept uncomfortably on either side as if margining the space of his safety. As I slept crosswise beneath their feet they could never stretch their legs, for whenever they did so they felt my little body and immediately shrank back frightened lest they push me off the bed. In spite of my few years, I sometimes could not sleep for lack of sufficient room. But when my parents got up to go to work, I could choose a better place, I and my brother being left on the bed to sleep all we wished.

Angelo M. Pellegrini, who became a professor of literature in the United States, described his childhood in Italy.

In 1912 we were a family of seven in Casabianca, a small community a few miles west of Florence, where we worked a bit of land as share-croppers. The children, of whom I was the third, ranged in age from two to fourteen years. The central, dominating fact of our existence was continuous, inadequately rewarded labor. It was not possible then, and is much less now, for a peasant to make an adequate living in Italy without owning his home and a few acres of land.

Education beyond the third grade was out of the question. The overwhelming majority of literate Italian immigrants in America would tell you, should you ask them, that they quit school after the third grade. It is not a matter of a magic number. At eight or nine years of age, if not sooner, the peasant child is old enough to bend his neck to the yoke and to fix his eyes upon the soil in which he must grub for bread. I did not

Farmers from outlying areas took their produce to towns to sell in the marketplace. For many immigrants, this was their only experience with urban life before leaving for America.

The real relatives are those inside the house.

If you want a happy life, stay away from your relatives.

Do not make your child better than you are.

—southern Italian proverbs

The town of Carrera, Italy, was famous for its high-quality marble, which was used for buildings and sculpture. Here, a team of oxen hauls slabs of marble to the Carrera railroad station in 1902.

know it then, but I know it now, that it is a cruel, man-made destiny from which there is yet no immediate hope of escape....

But misery to Father and Mother meant quite something else. I do not mean to imply that they saw—as I can see it now in retrospect—the real tragedy of our existence; nor that they had fancy notions about how the Pellegrinis should live. They were acutely aware of their responsibilities as parents; and they had some idea of the meaning of dignity in human life....They were outwardly stern when they refused the coin we needed to buy an ice-cream cone, and they tried to put the refusal in terms of some vague discipline; but they knew that they had refused because they did not have the coin. And that hurt them....

I was born in the incomparable Tuscan countryside, in the vicinity of Florence, in the shadow of the Leaning Tower of Pisa, outside the medieval walls of Lucca, amid olive groves and vineyards. I remember particularly the early autumns, when the leaves were beginning to fall and the earth to harden with the early frosts. I remember walking barefooted to school, under the bright skies of Indian summer, quickening the pace to traverse more rapidly the shaded portions of the path, looking intently at the wayside vines for that last, possible cluster of grapes which had escaped the sharp eye of the gleaners. How precious, when found, that last sweet cluster! The final taste of the grape until the next season should come!

And I remember the winters! The long winter evenings I remember, with the family and the neighbors huddled at the hearth, with only the illusion of a fire to keep us warm; and how we took turns blowing in the coals to start a flame which soon thereafter subsided into thin ringlets of smoke. How the peasants unleashed their morbid imaginations and summoned forth horrible stories about the spirits of evil. The singing I remember; the passing of the wine jug; the final retreat into dark, cold, damp rooms, to sleep several in a bed, between sheets of homespun, rough, almost thorny, linen.

And the spring and early summer I remember! Like the hibernating animal, the peasant subsists during the barren winter months on his own substance. When spring comes he returns again to the soil to gather the mushrooms, the tender shoots of the turnip, the succulent core of the chicory; then to spade and to rake and to sow, that later he may reap the fruit, the vegetables, the grain. I remember the anxiety with which we, sugar-hungry peasants, awaited the first melons, the first fruit on the tree, the first grape on the vine. Who, more acutely than the peasant, is aware of the intimate, personal significance of the miracle of life?...

All these things I remember. They were the excitement and the drama of my early years. But the experiences I remember most vividly were even more intimately related to my life as a peasant boy. I remember labor, unremitting toil, exalted in the home, in the church, in the school, and its necessity quickly realized by the growing child. I remember the stonecutters crushing rock by hand for the roadbed; the women in the fields hoeing, weeding, harvesting, and then rushing to the kitchen to prepare dinner for the family; the men setting out with their tools before the break of day; the bent grandmothers spinning, weaving, and tending the children for their daughters; the draymen hauling rock, hay, and sand from sunrise to sunset; and the venders, the beggars, the peddlers plying their trade in sun and rain....

At the age of seven I worked for wages. I hired out as a human disk harrow, an adolescent clod-buster. Barefooted and in abbreviated breeches, I went to a neighbor's field to pulverize the clods of earth with a wooden mallet. All for a nickel a day!...

During the autumn months I gathered fuel for the winter.... I also helped with the spading, the hoeing, the weeding, and—most pleasant of occupations—the harvest.

One Italian recalled the system of hiring fieldhands in southern Italy.

What was it like at that time? In the morning, when it was still dark, the *braccianti* [laborers] went to stand in the *piazza* [town square]. The *caporale* [foreman] looked at you with a sour face. There were always more men than he needed, so when he selected his workers no one ever asked either the rate of pay or the location. We understood the system; there was no need to be reminded. The job began at first light and continued through the day. On Sundays the *caporale* set up a table outside the door of the farmhouse and we would line up for our wages. "How long did you work?" he would ask. If you replied six days, he would correct you. "You are wrong—four days." "Why four?" you would ask. "Four," he would say. "You doubt my word? If you don't trust me, don't come to work." He would pay us for four days of work and would pocket the rest.

Charles Ferrara treasured this photo of his parents and three sisters, who remained in Sicily when he left for America in the early 20th century.

Giuseppe Garibaldi

One Italian statesman who was saddened by the emigration of his countrymen was Giuseppe Garibaldi. He called it a "significant evil," but he understood its causes and sympathized.

Garibaldi was born on July 4, 1807, the son of a seagoing family. As a young man he became a ship captain. His idealism led him to become involved with Giuseppe Mazzini in a plot to create an Italian republic in 1834. After it failed, Garibaldi escaped a death sentence by fleeing to South America.

During his years there—1836 to 1848—he gained an international reputation as a defender of liberty. Commanding a ship for Brazilians fighting for their own independence, he liberated African slaves from Portuguese ships crossing the Atlantic. He offered the slaves the choice of being set ashore or joining his forces. Many joined, and one of the Africans served as Garibaldi's second in command. It was at this time that Garibaldi formed his loyal band of Redshirts and gained the experience in guerrilla warfare that he would use later in Italy.

Garibaldi returned to Italy in 1848, leading the defense of the short-lived Roman Republic. He called for volunteers with the words, "All who have the name of Italy, not only on their lips, but in their hearts also...let them follow me!" However, Garibaldi was forced to abandon the city, and again he went into exile, this time in the United States.

Garibaldi developed a great admiration for the United States and its ideals. He took out an application for citizenship, and always regarded America as his second country. In fact, when the U.S. Civil War broke out, President Abraham Lincoln offered Garibaldi a commission as a general in the Union army. By this time, Garibaldi was involved in the liberation of Sicily and he could not accept Lincoln's offer. But many Italians who had already settled in the United States served in a special unit that they named in Garibaldi's honor.

Most emigrants took with them a deep respect for Garibaldi when they left Italy. Pictures of him could be found in the homes and shops of Italian enclaves in the United States. Italian Americans had a double celebration on July 4 —the Independence Day of their new country and the birthday of the greatest Italian patriot.

THE DREAM OF THE IMMIGRANTS

In the 1960s, Angelo Massari proudly wrote down the story of his life, beginning with his struggle to persuade his father to let him go to the United States.

Not very pleased with the shallow life of my little hometown [in Sicily] and with what went on there, and convinced that I had no future in the place, on reaching my thirteenth birthday I decided to emigrate. I had heard of America, but had only a very slight idea of what America was. Mine was possibly a childish aspiration, but I wanted to chain fortune to me, as others had done....

On the other hand, when I began thinking about America I had to settle with my father. When I told him what I had in mind, he did not know whether to laugh or to kick me on the seat of my pants. I kept insisting for four long years without weakening, for I was then, as I am now, persevering and steadfast.... At the same time, I was gathering all kinds of information about the country of my dreams. I used to interview people who had returned from America. I asked them a thousand questions, how America was, what they did in Tampa [where some of his relatives lived], what kind of work was to be had.... One of them told me that the language was English, and I asked him how to say one word or another in that language. I got these wonderful samples of a Sicilian-American English from him: tu sei un boia, gud, gud morni, olraiti [all right]...sciusi, bred, iessi, bud.... He told me also that in order to ask for work, one had to say, "Se misti gari giobbi for mi?"

All in all, when the American left I had stored together about thirty words of the new language.... And I kept pestering my father about my journey to America.

Pascal D'Angelo, who arrived in 1910, later described why Italians emigrated.

Our people have to emigrate. It is a matter of too much boundless life and too little space. We feel tied up there. Every bit of cultivable soil is owned by those fortunate few who lord over us. Before spring comes into our valley all the obtainable land is rented out or given to the peasants for a season under usurious conditions, namely, for three-fourths, one-half or one-fourth of the crops.... Up to a few years ago some peasants had to take land even on the one-fifth basis; that is, the man who worked the land and bought even seeds and manure would only get one-fifth of the harvest, while the owner who merely allowed him to use the land would receive four-fifths. This was possible up to a short while ago. But today such a thing is absolutely impossible since no peasant would agree to it unless his head were not functioning normally. And what is it that saves the man and keeps him from being ground under the hard power of necessity? The New World!

Previously, there was no escape; but now there is.... escape from the rich landowners, from the terrors of drought, from the specter of starvation, in the boundless Americas out of which at times people returned with fabulous tales and thousands of liras—riches unheard of before among peasants.

Rocco Boffilo, from Calabria, explained why he decided to emigrate.

Things go badly here. Many *contadini* [peasants] here do not eat bread. They live on potatoes and beans. The salaries have increased, that is true, but one can only find work three or four months out of the year. Why do so many go to America? Because they are better off there. The work here, in comparison, is too much to bear. Up at sunrise, carrying your tools while walking several kilometers to the fields and then returning during the darkness in the evening, totally exhausted: that is the life we live here. And add to that a long, frigid winter season. When someone returns from America to tell us that the wages are superior and that there are fewer discomforts, many of the men cannot resist the temptation to go and find out for themselves.

Stefano Miele, an Italian immigrant who came to the United States around the turn of the century, described the allure of America.

If I am to be frank, then I shall say that I left Italy and came to America for the sole purpose of making money.... I suffered no political oppression in Italy. I was not seeking political ideals: as a matter of fact, I was quite satisfied with those of my native land. If I could have worked my way up in my chosen profession in Italy, I would have stayed in Italy. But repeated efforts showed me that I could not. America was the land of opportunity, and so I came, intending to make money and then return to Italy. This is true of most Italian emigrants to America.

Rocco Morelli, an immigrant who arrived in the United States in 1920, remembered his mother telling him why they were leaving Italy.

I do not want to raise my children in this country any longer. I don't want wars. I don't want no poverty. I want to go to the United States. You work over there. The children will work over there. And at least we'll eat.

In 1902, flower sellers hawked their wares in the Street of Steps in Gradoni de Chioja, Naples. In the United States, Italian immigrants often continued to work in such familiar trades as a way of making a living.

An emigrant family preparing to board ship at Genoa in 1894. Genoa was the chief port from which emigrants from northern Italy left for America.

CHAPTER TWO

THE TRIP TO AMERICA

An Italian proverb states, *Chi esce riesce*—"He who leaves succeeds." But it took a great deal of courage for emigrants to leave the village where they had been born, to bid farewell to the *famiglia* that had been their only source of security and love, and to set out for a land that was little more than a legend to many peasants of the Mezzogiorno.

The first step involved contact with distrusted government officials: obtaining a *nulla osta*, a document that declared there were no legal restrictions to prevent a person from leaving the country. Often illiterate because work was of greater importance than school, the emigrants threaded their way through the bureaucratic process. In order to obtain a *nulla osta*, the village secretary had to issue a birth certificate, which was then submitted to the police headquarters in the provincial capital. A man's record was checked to see if he had completed his military service or was wanted for a crime.

When the required documents were in order, preparations for departure began. The village priest celebrated masses to ensure the safety and success of the emigrants. Members of the family loaded the emigrants down with food, clothing, and other things that might be necessary on the journey. When whole families left together, they sold their houses and everything else, in order to obtain as much money as possible for the uncertain venture that lay ahead.

Finally, the tearful farewells were said. On foot, on the backs of donkeys, or sometimes by train, the emigrants made their way to one of the ports on the seacoast where ships would take them across the ocean. For many arriving in Palermo, Naples, or Genoa, it was the first time they had ever seen a city.

There, they faced danger from swindlers and pickpockets. Many emigrants had to borrow money or sign labor contracts to obtain a ship ticket. Not understanding what they had signed, they bound themselves to a life of hard work before they had even left for the New World.

In the late 19th and early 20th century, the journey across the Atlantic in a steamship usually lasted about two weeks. It was the worst part of the trip, remembered by many as the *via dolorosa*, the "sorrowful way." Crammed into overcrowded berths stacked to the ceiling below decks, the immigrants breathed foul air, suffered from seasickness, contracted diseases, and continually feared that the ship would sink.

One emigrant noted that the sea passage "seems to have been so calculated as to inflict upon us the last, full measure of suffering and indignity, and to impress upon us for the last time that we were the 'wretched refuse' of the earth; to exact from us a final price for the privilege we hoped to enjoy in America."

Before 1870 few Italians made the decision to seek a new life across the ocean. In the 50 years after 1820, when immigration records first were kept, only about 25,000 Italians arrived in the United States. Most of them came from northern Italy. Some were artists, sculptors, and stoneworkers; Italians, known for their skill in these occupations, were in demand for such projects as the construction of the Capitol building in Washington, D.C. Others were political exiles, fleeing the turmoil of their homeland.

After 1870, the tide of Italians flowing toward the United States swelled to a flood. Between 1870 and 1920, more than 4 million arrived. More than 80 percent were from the Mezzogiorno, where poverty had made life unbearable. At first, the majority were men between the ages of 16 and 45. When some returned, displaying the wealth they had earned in America, the rush to the New World began.

Sometimes, whole villages departed at the same time. An Italian writing in 1902 reported that the peasants of a Sicilian village gathered one day in front of the feudal lord who owned the land on which they toiled. They threw down their shovels and posted a notice: "Sir, do your farming yourself—we are going to America."

BLAZING THE TRAIL

After returning from his trip in search of the Seven Cities of Cíbola, Brother Marco de Nizza worked to convert the native people to Christianity until his death in 1558. His trailblazing efforts paved the way for future Spanish settlements in the southwestern United States.

Italian explorers and missionaries were among the earliest Europeans to journey to what is now the United States. Like Columbus and the other discoverers, they worked in the service of other European countries. Among the first to arrive were Marco de Nizza, Enrico Tonti, and Eusebio Chino.

Brother Marco de Nizza's eyewitness report of the fabled Seven Golden Cities of Cíbola inspired a treasure hunt for two centuries. Born around 1492 in the city of Nizza (today part of France and called Nice), Marco joined the Franciscan order as a young man. In 1531 he went to the New World as a missionary. Eight years later, in Mexico City, he met the conquistador Francisco Coronado, who had heard tales of treasure-laden cities somewhere in the north.

Brother Marco agreed to lead a scouting party. On March 7, 1539, accompanied by Estevanico—an African slave who had already been on a harrowing six-year journey from Florida to Texas—Marco set out with some Native American guides. They traveled into present-day Arizona, where other natives told them about the rich city of Cíbola.

Leaving Brother Marco behind, Estevanico went to find the city. Some days later a messenger arrived with the sad news that Estevanico had been killed. Nevertheless, Brother Marco pressed on. His report described what he found.

Cíbola...is situated on a plain at the foot of a round hill.... The houses are...all made of stone with diverse stories, and flat roofs.... The people are somewhat white...have Emeralds and other jewels, although they esteem none so much as turquoises, with which they adorn the walls of the porches of their houses...and they use them instead of money.... They use vessels of gold and silver, for they have no other metal, whereof there is greater use and more abundance than in Peru.... When I told the chief men what a goodly city Cíbola seemed to me, they answered me that it was the least of the seven cities, and that Totonteac is the greatest and best of them all, because it has so many houses and people that there is no end of them.... I made a great heap of stones by the help of the Indians, and on the top thereof I set up a small slender cross....

[Brother Marco wanted to get a look at the other cities, and traveled to the plain where they stood.] At the entrance of this plain I saw...seven Towns...which were afar off in a low valley being very green and a most fruitful soil, out of which ran many Rivers. I was informed that there was much gold in this valley, and that the inhabitants work it into vessels and thin plates.... And from thence I returned on my voyage with as much haste as I could make.

Hearing Brother Marco's report, Coronado immediately set out with more than 1,000 men to find the seven cities. Over the next two years his expedition marched as far north as Kansas, searching in vain for the fabled cities of gold.

Born around 1650 in the northern Italian city of Gaeta, Enrico Tonti enlisted in the French army when he was 18. His military career ended when his right hand was destroyed by a grenade. For the rest of his life, he wore a metal claw on the end of his wrist.

In 1679, Tonti joined Robert Cavelier de La Salle's expedition to the New World. Landing in Quebec, La Salle and his men threaded their way up the St. Lawrence River and through the Great Lakes. After reaching the Illinois River near present-day Chicago, La Salle decided to follow its course to see if it led to the Mississippi River.

La Salle went back to Canada to obtain more supplies. While he was gone, Tonti befriended the chief of an Illinois tribe, who dubbed him "iron-hand." When a scout reported the approach of a hostile group of Iroquois, Tonti went alone to meet them, carrying a necklace as a gift. He later recalled:

When I had come upon them, these wretches seized me, took the necklace from my hand, and one of them reaching through the crowd, plunged a knife through my breast, wounding a rib near the heart. However, having recognized me, they carried me into the midst of their camp and...held a council...There was a man behind me with a knife in his hand, who every now and then lifted up my hair. They were divided in opinion. [One chief] wished positively to have me burnt. [Another,] a friend of M. de La Salle, wished to have me set at liberty. He carried his point. They...sent me to deliver [a] message to the Illinois. I had much difficulty in reaching them on account of the great quantity of blood I had lost, both from my wound and from my mouth.

After Tonti recovered, he rejoined La Salle, who had outfitted an expedition of 50 men. In January 1682, they reached the point where the Illinois River meets the Mississippi. Building six canoes, the explorers floated downriver for four months, finally reaching the delta where the Mississippi flows into the Gulf of Mexico. They were the first Europeans to make the journey. La Salle claimed the vast region for the king of France, naming it Louisiana.

In 1687, King Louis XIV granted Tonti the rights to the Louisiana fur trade. Building a fort 150 miles north of St. Louis, Tonti explored much of the vast Mississippi Valley during the next 20 years. In 1704, he contracted yellow fever and died at the French outpost in Mobile. More than two centuries later, Italian immigrants in Arkansas would name their settlement Tontitown after this New World pioneer.

Enrico Tonti with a Native American guide in east Texas, as painted by Bruce Marshall in 1973.

During the 30 years from his arrival to his death in 1711, Father Eusebio Chino established more than 20 mission churches in Mexico and Arizona. San Xavier del Bac, near Tucson, Arizona, is one that remains standing today. Chino also planted grapevines and brought the first cattle, horses, sheep, and goats to the region.

SAYING GOOD-BYE

Taking the advice of l'Americano, *a neighbor who had prospered in the United States and returned to Italy, the father of Angelo Pellegrini left for America in 1912. For many months, his wife and children in Italy heard nothing from him. As Angelo recalled:*

We were terribly worried. I remember that Mother, notwithstanding her effort to keep the family cheerful, was gradually breaking under the burden of fear. From day to day we expected a black-bordered letter which would bring us news of Father's death. We had resigned ourselves to the worst. But when our friend the postman, who knew well Father's handwriting, came whistling merrily to the door, and holding something behind his back, we knew that all was well. All was well indeed!

Father was very much alive! The letter contained an eloquent description of the new home he had found for us in the state of Washington. "Sell immediately everything we own and leave on the first available ship out of Genoa. Money for the passage will be sent within a week."

Within twenty-four hours the Casabianca neighbors had heard that the Pellegrini family was going to America. And what did it mean to them or to us?... Generations of them had lived and died without having gone even so far as Florence, about twenty miles away. During the days preceding our departure they clustered about us, incredulous, dazed, eager to help with the preparations, and repeated over and over, *So you are going to America!* Yes, we are going to America to join our father. Beyond the simple fact that America was a sort of fairyland and that we were going to Father, we had no idea of what was in store for us.

After trying for four years, 17-year-old Angelo Massari finally persuaded his father to pay his way to America.

Everything was ready for my departure, and I was anxiously waiting for the arrival of the great day. For several weeks I had seen an occasional trace of tears in my mother's eyes, but she tried her best to hide her sorrow from me, while I, on my part, tried to ignore the evidence that she had been crying....

On the eve of my departure, I wrote with white chalk and in large letters on the inside postern of my balcony: *13 Ottobre 1902.* My good mother preserved that sign for many years, for it had been written by her son. That evening she could not keep back her tears, and she cried like a child. I will never forget those tears and my good mother.

How crowded my home was that evening! Relatives and

Emigrants aboard a ship wave good-bye to friends and relatives on shore as they leave the port of Naples in 1935. The woman with the handkerchief, Rosa Camillo, moved to Milwaukee. She never saw her parents again.

friends flocked in. I thanked them for their good wishes, trying to be as calm as possible, hiding behind a stern front the commotion that was in my heart....

About 10:30 p.m. a man came to tell me that the carts were ready. The saddening moment had arrived....

I went down the stairs and on the threshold my good mother hugged me and kissed me again and again. Her last words were, "God speed you, my dear son. God will always be with you. Write me as soon as possible and write me always."

All our neighbors were at their windows, on balconies, or in front of their doors, and all were saying: "Good voyage, Angelo, and good luck. Do not forget to write when you land in America."

Mary Nick Juliano recalled leaving the little town of San Giovanni in Fiore, Calabria, 74 years before.

I t's still a vivid dream. I remember the old cobblestone road—just an old road. We lived down there with my grandmother, my mother's mother, Serafina Sucurro.... There was a little scene in front of our home there in Italy that I'll never forget. I hung on to Grandma Sucurro, and that's just as vivid as today. I wouldn't let go! It took two or three to unwrap my little arms. I was just five! And I screamed her name. My uncle grabbed me and hugged me tight. And the last thing I remember—is—that dear, dear little grandma, falling on the cobblestone road, screaming my name.

Parting produced emotional scenes at railroad stations. Angelo Mosso was on a train that stopped at Castrofilippo, Sicily, in March 1905. He described the departure.

The stationmaster told me that thirty emigrants were departing including seven women. They had been waiting for two months for a ship, and last week they received word to go to Palermo for embarkation. When the train began to move, a piercing cry arose from the crowd along the platform. Each person had an arm upraised clutching a handkerchief. One woman broke away from the crowd and began to run alongside the train as it pulled out of the station, yelling out: "Say hello to him (meaning her husband); remind him that I am still waiting for him to send me the money for the steamship ticket. Tell him I am waiting, and tell him...tell him...that if I have to stay here any longer I will die."

The unwary emigrant could be separated from his life's savings at the port of embarkation, as in this 1898 description of Genoa.

Once the emigrants decide to leave home, they find themselves burdened with all sorts of unanticipated expenses, including the special trains that transport hundreds of them each day to Genoa, and the cost of food and lodging. The [ticket] agents systematically fleece their charges. They are sent here a week before their sailing and are directed to those merchants and innkeepers with whom the agents have arranged a sharing of the spoils. For twenty years now, this city has had to endure the spectacle of large groups of pathetic and famished emigrants, devoid of decent clothing and money, in the most immoral circumstances, stretched out wherever they can— on the floors of hotels, on the streets, in public places—and they are to be seen everywhere, day and night.

CAV. JOHN FOSTER CARR

GUIDA

DEGLI STATI UNITI

PER

L'IMMIGRANTE ITALIANO

PUBBLICATA A CURA
DELLA
SOCIETA' DELLE FIGLIE DELLA RIVOLUZIONE AMERICANA
SEZIONE DI CONNECTICUT.

The Immigrant Education Society in New York published this guidebook for Italian immigrants.

FROM VILLAGE TO PORT

To board a ship for America, the emigrants had to get to a port city. Naples was the busiest. An emigrant who left in 1900 with five members of his family describes the first leg of his journey to Naples via Palermo.

We left in a two-wheeled cart that carried a big home-made trunk, my mother, two of my brothers, my sister and also a cousin....On our way to Palermo, which was forty miles away, we had a horse and driver. We stayed overnight in a small town where we slept in a stable; the horse slept on the hay. After we got to Palermo I remember that we hopped onto a small launch—there was no such thing as a dock.

The Mediterranean was very rough and we had to travel some distance to get to the ship. It took all night. And I remember so well that there was really a lot of crying going on because of the frightfulness of the Mediterranean. The boat was not a boat to come across the ocean. You had to go to Naples—and there you took the ship.

Angelo Massari began his journey to America in 1902, when he was 17.

There were seven of us leaving Santo Stefano that evening....As soon as we took our places in the carts, the caravan moved on....It was not yet daylight when we reached Lercara Bassa, and we had to wait two hours for the express to Palermo. When the train arrived, we got on board, and it then left for the capital of Sicily.

It was the first time I had ridden on a train, and I got the impression from its speed that the world was revolving around us. We reached Cefalu and then Termini Imeresi, where I saw the sea for the first time. I had never thought that the sea was so immense, and I was really impressed....We had two days to rest in Palermo.

Going through the city I felt lost. I looked at the streets, at the palaces, and at the crowds with a sense of wonder. All in all, it was a wonderful spectacle....

[A boat took him from Palermo to Naples, where] we had to undergo a medical examination, but chiefly of the eyes. Those who were found sound and sane, and without any infection in their eyes, were passed. The unfit were rejected and left behind.

We spent a day near the pier, and I had my shoes shined in the Piazza del Porto [the harbor's plaza]. A man sitting alongside me was also getting a shine. I asked him where he came from. He answered, "America."... He told me that he had returned to Naples because things had not gone well with him in the New World. I listened to him, thinking at the same time that here was a man who had seen the New World and was not satisfied with it, while here was I leaving for the new country without knowing what was going to happen to me....

While waiting for sailing time I was taken through the city in a carriage. In a very wide street, probably the Corso Toledo, I saw, to my great surprise, a carriage that was moving without horses. It was the dawn of the automobile in its primitive and imperfect form. If somebody had told me at that moment that nine years later I would own an automobile, one of the best on the American market, I would not have believed him.

Nineteen-year-old Totonno Pappatore left his village, Alberobello, in the heart of Italy's Puglia region, in 1906. He kept a journal of his trip to America.

At 6:40 in the morning I left the house and walked through the village to the railroad station. Only my brother Scipione accompanied me.... I had not made a point of telling anyone of my departure, so it was with some surprise that I discovered many of my friends waiting to see me off at the station.

Eleven young men were leaving. It was a beautiful day, and the parting was joyful and without unusual strain.... Our arrival at Naples was not pleasant. It was pouring when we left the station for the hotel. Our earlier enthusiasm was quickly dampened not only by the chilling rain, but also by the condition of the city.... The filth and congestion are terrible here. Entire families live out their miserable lives crowded into a single room. The buildings are dilapidated and the streets resemble a dung heap. The garbage is swept into large piles and burned where it stands. To add to the misery of this place, Vesuvius is in a state of eruption and volcanic ash is everywhere....

Once at the hotel we found ourselves in the hands of the shipping company that would hereafter be responsible for our welfare. With the many other emigrants awaiting transport, we were herded into a dining hall for a tasteless, hurried supper, and then, we were left to arrange ourselves as best we could for the night. I was the only one with a bed of my own.

[The next day, they received inoculations and physical examinations.]

On April 29th, as we were making final preparations to board the ship *Bulgaria*, I realized with a sinking feeling that my billfold, which had contained 50 lire, was no longer in my pocket. We looked everywhere but it was gone. I finally had to accept the fact that it must have been taken from me while we were going through the final inspection, and that I will now have to depend on my friends for money until we reach America.

Waiting at the dock to board a ship, these immigrants are surrounded by bundles containing everything they own. Leaving their home villages, often for the first time in their lives, was a decision that required great courage.

Josephine Orlando Saiia of Greenfield, Wisconsin, had a recipe for mustasole, *or "hard cookie," which many emigrants took along on the ocean voyages:*

This recipe sustained many immigrants on their voyage to Ellis Island and their new homes. Travelers would order suitcases full of these cookies to eat on board as the dining rooms were too expensive. They are very, very hard when dry and become chewy when damp—like [on] an ocean voyage. They do not spoil, can be eaten for a year, keep well with no crumbs. Pack well. I have one that's fifty years old. These are made by special bakers and were often made in fancy shapes—animals, flowers, baskets, etc., and sold as gifts at festivals.

We came from Cosenza, Italy. My grandfather came through Ellis Island with these cookies many times between late 1890's and World War I. My father came in 1906, made many trips. Then served in the U.S. Army in WWI and became a citizen, so when mother and I came in March 1926, we did not go through Ellis Island because we were listed as "returning to U.S.A." Because we were citizens, we were taken off the ship before it docked at Ellis Island.

INGREDIENTS

3 cups sifted all-purpose flour (in bowl)

1 1/2 cups sifted all-purpose flour (in cup)

1 1/2 cups melted honey, warm

1 1/4 tsp. vanilla

or lemon flavor

Place 3 cups flour in bowl, add hot honey, salt, flavor and mix well. Add more flour to make very stiff dough, knead on board till smooth. Place in bowl and cover and let rest for at least 12 hours, *not* in refrigerator. Divide in 4 pieces—knead each till smooth, using little flour. Shape as you would children's clay— build on ungreased cookie sheets—add little oil on top and shine, or water to make it stick. Bake at 325 degrees for 15 or 20 minutes (gas or electric varies) till golden brown. Remove from pan while hot and lay on flat surface to harden. (Limp when hot—*hard* when cold.) No crumbs.

THE OCEAN VOYAGE

An Italian author, Edmondo De Amicis, sailed to the United States in 1890. He described the crowd boarding the ship Galileo *at the port of Genoa.*

Workmen, peasants, women with children at the breast, little fellows with the tin medal of the infant asylum still hanging around their necks passed on their way, and almost everyone was carrying something. They had folding chairs, they had bags and trunks of every shape in their hands or on their heads; their arms were full of mattresses and bedclothes, and their berth tickets were held fast in their mouths. Poor mothers that had a child for each hand carried their bundles with their teeth. Old peasant women in wooden shoes, holding up their skirts so as not to stumble over the cleats of the gangplank, showed bare legs that were like sticks. Many were barefoot and had their shoes hung around their necks....

Then, suddenly, a stoppage of the procession and, amid a shower of blows and curses, a drove of cattle or a flock of sheep came along; and when they were got on board, all frightened and struggling here and there, they mingled their bellowing and their bleating and the neighing of the horses in the forward part of the ship, with the cries of sailors and porters, and with the stunning clatter of the donkey engine that was hoisting in whole piles of packing cases....

Suddenly furious cries were heard from the passport office, and people were seen running that way. It proved to be a peasant with a wife and four children—all found by the examining physician to have the itch. The first few questions had shown the man to be out of his mind; and, on being refused a passage, he had broken out into frenzy....

At last the sailors were heard shouting fore and aft, "*Chi non e passeggero, a terra*"—"All ashore that's going ashore."

These words sent a thrill from one end of the *Galileo* to the other. In a few moments all strangers were out of the ship, the bridge was hauled ashore, and fasts cast off, the entering port closed, a whistle sounded, and the ship began to move. Then women burst out crying, youths who had been laughing grew serious, and bearded men hitherto stolid were seen to pass a hand across their eyes....A few persons who had just reached the wharf had only time to fling some bundles of cigars or some oranges on board. These were duly caught but some of the last ones fell into the water. Lights began to twinkle in the city. The ship slid softly along through the darkness of the harbor almost furtively, as it were, as if she were carrying off a cargo of kidnapped human flesh.

In 1913, nine-year-old Angelo Pellegrini, with his mother, brothers, and sisters, boarded the ship Taormina, *bound from Genoa to New York. Four decades later, Angelo recalled:*

It was a rough passage made the more terrifying by ugly rumors. Peasants who did not understand why some objects sink and others float...had to accept on faith the phenomenon of a floating ship. Their faith, of course, was severely taxed. Every time the ship rolled, or dropped groaning into the trough of a wave, accompanied by the clatter of falling tin dishes with which each steerage passenger had been provided, she was presumed to go down.

I remember, with lingering traces of horror, one particularly terrifying moment. For several hours the ship had been lunging uncertainly, the heavy water splitting against the bow, sweeping over it, and reuniting in a mass of foam and spray on the foredeck. With every thrust forward she seemed to be driven back by the watery walls which the wind raised across her path. Then she apparently got astride a mountainous wave which lifted her higher and higher, as if a reversed gravity were hoisting her into the sky. She paused for what seemed an interminable instant upon the crest. Then, bow foremost, she plunged down, down, down, propellers screaming in the air, the water rising on both sides, the crash of dishes and baggage mingling with the shrieks of the steerage passengers. What had happened? No one knew. There were rumors that the propellers had broken; that the engine had exploded; that we were drifting in the Atlantic with death our destination....

Most of [the passengers] were southern Italians who had come aboard at Naples. Apparently out of habit, the men carried their jackets in the crook of the arm—as if they were about to go somewhere. The women were hooded in black shawls.

The steerage below decks, where most immigrants ate and slept, was stifling and crowded. Whenever the weather was good, people gathered on deck for fresh air.

At the embarkation point, friends and family often watched the emigrants leave. Luciano De Cresenzo remembered a farewell custom:

Many immigrants had brought on board balls of yarn, leaving one end of the line with someone on land. As the ship slowly cleared the dock, the balls unwound amid the farewell shouts of the women, the fluttering of the handkerchiefs, and the infants held high. After the yarn ran out, the long strips remained airborne, sustained by the wind, long after those on land and those at sea had lost sight of each other.

A crowd boards a ship in Genoa around 1898. Many voyagers took along bread, salami, and cheese to sustain themselves on the journey.

Some of them stood or knelt in the posture of prayer. Frequently someone screamed an invocation to San Gennaro, their patron saint. Day after day, for three long weeks, the scene never changed: the same faces, pale with sickness and with fear, stared vacantly, or cast furtive glances at one another, as if each sought reassurance in the presence of his doomed companions. An elderly woman...complained of her misery to a member of the crew. When he assured her that she would not die she shot back at him, with unintended humor, that he had taken from her her last hope.

Guido Gallucci traveled in steerage with his sister in 1907. They had a surprise when they saw their sleeping quarters.

In the middle of the room, where some bunks had been taken away, there was a closed stall about four feet high and in it was a horse!...This animal belonged to a rich American who was in first class and this was the only place they could find room for him. All this was very puzzling because most Italian ships have a government representative on board as the law required. There was such a man but he seemed to think it was a great joke, so I guess he must have been paid to allow it.

So the horse was with us while we slept and while we ate. He was a nervous horse, and he stomped a lot and neighed and made funny noises all the time except when it was dark.

Francesco Ventresca sailed from Naples on the French liner La Champagne, *carrying salami and cheese in his suitcase. He described the steerage experience.*

There were over a thousand of us on board. I recall only steerage. I did not venture to speculate on higher living. Most of us were assigned to bunks—berths would be too refined a name for them. Some of the men were placed one story below the deck and others two stories below. We managed to get a bit of light through the hatchway or through the portholes. No one could stay below for very long. We were all the time on deck, except at night and in stormy weather—and we had plenty of that.

We ate three meals a day in groups of six. One man was

given a big pan and he got the food while we looked for a good spot on deck. We just crouched or squatted like the Orientals. We could not very well say that we enjoyed the food, for only genuine hunger could have made it palatable, and in this case hunger was the best sauce.

Totonno Pappatore noted in his diary the terror of a storm.

The big event of our voyage across the turbulent Atlantic was a terrifying night storm. The huge waves bounced our ship around like a cork in a vat of fermenting wine. We were knocked from pillar to post; persons were thrown from their bunks; the women were petrified, and cried, screamed, and prayed all at the same time.

An orphan, Rocco Corresca grew up on the streets of Naples. One day he met a young man who showed him a handful of gold and said that he had earned it with a few days' work in America. The man got Rocco and a friend work in the boiler room of a ship bound for America. Years later, Rocco remembered:

We had to carry coal to the place where it could be thrown on the fires. Francesco and I were very sick from the great heat at first and lay on the coal for a long time, but they threw water on us and made us get up. We could not stand on our feet well, for everything was going around and we had no strength. We said that we wished we had stayed in Italy no matter how much gold there was in America. We could not eat for three days and could not do much work. Then we got better and sometimes we went up above and looked about. There was no land anywhere and we were much surprised. How could the people tell where to go when there was no land to steer by?

We were so long on the water that we began to think we should never get to America or that, perhaps, there was not any such place, but at last we saw land and came up to New York.

On some of the immigrant ships, the passengers assembled on deck for meals. Crew members served soup from metal tanks along with a piece of stale bread. The food was only enough to keep the immigrants alive until they reached port.

Immigrants like this family had to take a ferry to Ellis Island after leaving their ships in New York Harbor. Photographer Lewis Hine, who captured this scene, wrote, "Sometimes...they waited for several days and nights before the little ferry boat could bring them to the island."

CHAPTER THREE

LAMERICA

The most thrilling part of the journey was the first sight of "Lamerica," as many Italians called it. For most, that was the Statue of Liberty, with its torch held high to show the way to "the Golden Door." More than 95 percent of all Italian immigrants followed in the wake of Giovanni da Verrazano, arriving in New York City. They passed through the Narrows between Brooklyn and Staten Island, where a great bridge now stands named in Verrazano's honor. The very first emigrants to make the voyage from Italy to New York, in 1657, were a group of Italian Protestants who went to the Dutch colony of New Amsterdam to escape religious persecution.

In the earliest years of immigration, the newcomers simply filed down the gangplank of the ship into the streets of the nation's largest city. They were immediately surrounded by "runners" from boardinghouses and travel agencies. Each runner quoted low rates for the services of his employer—but very often, the unwary immigrants later learned that they had "misunderstood." Unless they paid what was demanded, the police would be called. That threat was enough to intimidate the new-

comers into turning over their carefully hoarded funds.

In 1855, because so many unwary immigrants fell prey to these swindlers, New York State officials opened a landing station in an old fort called Castle Garden. Here, the new arrivals could exchange their foreign money at honest rates, buy railroad tickets to other destinations, and obtain information about lodging and employment from social agencies.

As the stream of immigrants grew ever larger in the late 19th century, the emphasis shifted from helping the newcomers to looking for their defects. In 1890 the federal government took over the immigration process. On January 1, 1892, Ellis Island immigration station opened. Here, in what Italians called *isola della lacrime* (the Island of Tears), uniformed officials examined the immigrants to weed out the sick, the lame, those without sufficient funds, and anyone else who seemed likely to be a "burden" on the United States.

From the time Ellis Island opened until 1924, when a new law severely restricted immigration, about 12 million people passed through its gates. Nearly one-third were Italians. The process was confusing, humiliating, and often frightening.

An ocean liner of the time could hold as many as 6,000 passengers. The ship docked to allow the first- and second-class passengers to depart. The steerage passengers who pressed against the rail were pushed back until the lucky ones left. Then they were herded down the gangplank into small ferryboats that would take them to the Island of Tears.

Here, only a mile of water separated them from America, but some would be rejected and never permitted ashore. A cough, a limp, or slowness of speech might be enough to send a hopeful immigrant on the 3,000-mile journey back to Italy.

At Ellis Island, the newcomers were separated into groups of 30; each had a number pinned to their coat or dress as identification. They moved through the large doors into a baggage area, up a stairway, and into the enormous Registry Hall. A constant din added to the confusion—babies crying, people shouting to each other in a dozen languages, and inspectors calling for each new group to approach.

Metal railings divided the floor, funneling the immigrants from one inspector to another. An official watched carefully any women carrying children. If the child appeared to be older than two years, the official made the mother put it down to prove it could walk.

A series of doctors checked each immigrant for certain diseases. Interpreters assisted the doctors in asking questions. Giulio Miranda reported, "In the doctor's hand was a piece of chalk; on the coats of about two out of every ten or eleven immigrants who passed him he scrawled a large white letter H for possible heart trouble, L for lameness, a circled X for suspected mental defects, or F for a bad rash on the face." Those with such chalk marks were sent away for closer examination.

The worst part of the medical exam came from the "eye men." Using a metal instrument, they pried back the eyelids of each immigrant, looking for a disease called trachoma. Any sign of this brought a chalked "E" (for "eye") on the clothing, bringing almost certain rejection.

The criteria the examiners used to judge an immigrant's fitness were hardly scientific. For example, the manual that guided the inspectors who examined immigrants for signs of mental illness listed "slow speech, low voice, trembling articulation, sad faces, tearful eyes, perplexity, difficulty in thinking" as symptoms. Under such conditions, it is amazing that anyone passed through the exami-

nations. But, remarkable, only about 2 percent of the new arrivals were sent back to Italy.

Sometimes, a single member of a family failed to pass the test. It might be a mother or father; their other relatives then faced the

Keeping their precious possessions with them, immigrants followed the long lines from one examiner to the next at Ellis Island. This is the dreaded eye exam.

choice of proceeding without them, or returning to Italy together. Such decisions were heartbreaking, for the unity of the family was of paramount value for Italians. And yet they might have sold all their possessions, sacrificing everything for

this one trip, this chance for success. Returning meant a life of utter poverty, abandonment of all hope. Parents judged unfit sometimes sent their healthy children to the ferries that would take them ashore, hoping that a friend or relative would be waiting there as promised, to help and shelter them.

Others were detained for days while awaiting further examination. The facilities for those staying overnight or longer were crowded. On an average night in 1907, 1,700 women and children were crowded into a dormitory built for 600. Some detainees tried desperately to swim to the New Jersey shore; few succeeded in that attempt, and their bodies were disposed of in a crematorium on Ellis Island.

Those who did pass the physical examinations now filed down the seemingly never-ending passageways to the final inspector. In a two-minute period (prescribed by the manual), the inspector barked out 38 questions: Where are you going? Do you have a job? What kind of work can you do? Is anyone waiting to meet you? How much money do you have?

The answers were not easy. In 1885 and 1887, Congress passed laws prohibiting immigrants who had signed work contracts in other countries from entering the United States. Those who were thought likely to become "public charges" (welfare recipients) were also banned. So it was wrong to say you already had a job, but equally wrong to say you did not. In addition, the government required immigrants to have a certain sum of money with them; the amount varied between $20 and $40.

If all these questions received satisfactory answers, the inspector glanced at the number pinned on the immigrant's clothing. Matching it with the list of ship's passengers, he wrote it down on an approval form. If the name was too long or unfamiliar or contained many vowels, as Italian names often did, the harried inspector might shorten or change it. At this point, some Italians received new, "American" names. It did not matter, for once they reached shore they were free to call themselves whatever they wished.

Clutching their suitcases, the immigrants were directed to one of three stairways, called the "Stairs of Separation." Those who had come in a group with others from the same village sometimes said goodbye here for the last time. One staircase was designated "New York Outsides." Those who climbed it had proved that a sponsor was awaiting them; they took the ferry that brought them to the southern tip of Manhattan Island. A second stairway was for "New York Detained." It led to holding pens where people waited for the arrival of sponsors. The third was for "Railroads," those who were traveling to another part of the United States. A ferry would take these newcomers to the railroad station at Hoboken, New Jersey.

Even this rigorous examination was not enough to satisfy those

This group of Italian immigrants has disembarked from the ship in the background. By the 1880s, steamships had almost entirely replaced wooden sailing ships like this one.

Americans who felt that large-scale immigration was a threat. Henry Cabot Lodge, who served as a U.S. congressman and senator for 30 years, wrote in 1891, "The condition of a large mass of the laboring population in the city of New York is enough to alarm every thinking man; and this dreadful condition of things is intensified every day by the steady inflow of immigration."

The outbreak of World War I in Europe in 1914 reduced the arrival of immigrants until the war ended four years later. But now the nativists, those legislators who opposed immigration, gained a majority in Congress. In 1921, a temporary federal law limited the number of immigrants allowed to enter the United States. Three years after that, a more comprehensive law set a limit of 150,000 European immigrants each year. Each country's quota was 2 percent of its proportion of the U.S. population in 1890. This gave preference to the groups that had arrived earlier. Those in the later wave of immigration, including Italians and Jews, were severely restricted by the new law.

From 1924 until the end of World War II in 1945, Italian immigration slowed to between 5,000 and 6,000 entries each year. The Golden Door has opened wider in the years since then, particularly after a 1965 law eliminated national immigration quotas. However, of the nearly 15 million Americans in the 1990 census who identified their ancestry as Italian, the great majority either came through Ellis Island or were descendants of those who did. That was the beginning of the Italian American experience.

EARLY ARRIVALS

In 1979, the United States issued a post-card with Francesco Vigo's portrait, in recognition of his contributions to winning the Revolutionary War in the Northwest. A county in Indiana is today named after Vigo.

Filippo Mazzei returned to Europe in 1785. He wrote James Madison, "I am about to depart, but my heart remains behind.... I know that wherever I go I shall always work for the well-being and progress of the country of my adoption."

Although relatively few Italians came to the United States before the 1870s, many of the earliest immigrants made important contributions to their adopted land.

Francesco Vigo, a native of Mondavi, Italy, arrived in New Orleans in 1774 when he was 30. By the time the American Revolution broke out, Vigo was a prosperous fur trader. His heart was with the Patriot cause. He used his own money to buy supplies for George Rogers Clark, who had raised a military force to capture English forts in the Northwest.

In December 1778 Vigo was captured while on his way to Vincennes, in what is now Indiana. The British governor released him after Vigo promised to do nothing harmful to British interests "on his way to St. Louis." True to his word, Vigo went to St. Louis. However, he continued on to Clark's headquarters to report that the fort at Vincennes was lightly defended. Clark swiftly led 200 men across the territory and captured Vincennes on February 24, 1779. It was a stunning defeat for the British.

Vigo's generosity earned him nothing except the honor of citizenship. Congress refused to repay him the money he had advanced to Clark. Years later, now in his seventies and virtually penniless, Vigo heard that Clark had been honored by his Kentucky neighbors. Vigo wrote him:

Permit an old man who has witnessed your exertions in behalf of your country in its revolutionary struggles, to address you.... I often thought that I had reasons to lament that the...services of the best patriots of those days were too easily forgotten.... But when I saw that on July 4th last the citizens of Jefferson County [Kentucky]...had paid an unfeigned tribute to the veteran to whose skill America and Kentucky owe so much...my sentiments chimed in unison....

Please, Sir, to accept this plain but genuine offering from a man whom you honored once with your friendship, and who will never cease to put up prayers to Heaven that the evening of your days may be serene and happy.

VIGO

"All men are created equal," wrote Thomas Jefferson in the Declaration of Independence. These famous words echoed a phrase written by his friend, the Italian Filippo Mazzei. Born in 1730 near Florence, Italy, Mazzei became a wine merchant in London in 1756. Benjamin Franklin, a visitor from America who shared Mazzei's interest in science, persuaded Mazzei to go to Virginia and plant Mediterranean grapes.

Mazzei soon became inspired by the growing spirit of independence. He wrote articles in the Virginia Gazette *that Jefferson translated into English. In one, Mazzei declared:*

All men are by nature equally free and independent. Such equality is necessary in order to create a free government.... A true Republican government cannot exist unless all men from the richest to the poorest are perfectly equal in their natural rights.

Jefferson certainly had these words in mind when he penned the Declaration of Independence in June 1776. He sent a handwritten copy of the document to Mazzei.

From 1855 till 1879, Constantino Brumidi, an Italian immigrant artist, decorated the U.S. Capitol with his work. Born in Rome in 1805, Brumidi arrived in New York when he was 47. His talent won him the offer to become chief artist for the new Capitol building—at $8 a day. Brumidi readily accepted and spent the rest of his life at the task. As he later wrote:

I have no longer any desire for fame or fortune. My one ambition and my daily prayer is that I may live long enough to make beautiful the Capitol of the one Country in the World in which there is liberty.

Brumidi painted frescoes on walls and ceilings, designed bronze staircases, and created marble statues. President Abraham Lincoln insisted that the work continue through the Civil War, saying, "If the world sees this Capitol going on they will know that we intend the Union shall go on." To paint the 4,664-square-foot mural on the interior of the Capitol dome, Brumidi lay on his back, 180 feet above the floor, for nearly two years.

When Brumidi was 75, while working just below the dome, an accident put an end to his work. Six weeks later, Brumidi sent a petition to Congress, reporting what happened.

Your petitioner, C. Brumidi...while sitting upon a temporary scaffold...the chair turned from under him and threw him over. He caught the round [rung] of a ladder and remained suspended by the strength of his arms for the space of 15 minutes.... A miraculous escape...was effected but the fright and shock to the nerves of your petitioner...now prevents him from constant work upon the scaffold but he is able and desirous...to continue work in his studio....

Your petitioner respectfully requests that the Honorable Committee will cause his name to be again placed upon the regular Payroll of Capitol employees....

The petitioner hopes to obtain this benefit as a reward of the long life spent in the service of the government.

C. Brumidi

Brumidi died five months later. Congress paid $200 for his funeral expenses. His memorial is his work. Visitors who look closely can see his proud signature on the murals: "C. Brumidi, Artist, Citizen of the U.S."

Lorenzo Da Ponte

Born in Venice in 1747, Lorenzo Da Ponte gained fame for writing the words for three of the operas composed by Wolfgang Amadeus Mozart. Da Ponte came to the United States in 1804. He was a tireless promoter of Italian culture, becoming the first professor of Italian language and literature at Columbia University. In 1825, Da Ponte took a group of his pupils to one of the first U.S. opera performances, *The Barber of Seville*. He wrote, "That admirable music caught them up, along with the rest of the audience, into a sort of ecstatic spell. [I] observed from their perfect silence, the expressions on their faces and in their eyes, and their constant clapping of hands, the marvelous effect that music had had on them." In 1833, with the help and financial contributions of other Italian immigrants, Lorenzo Da Ponte's great dream was realized. He opened the first opera house in New York. It began a musical tradition that has remained part of American culture.

Constantino Brumidi worked on the U.S. Capitol through the administrations of six presidents, from Franklin Pierce to Rutherford B. Hayes. In a eulogy to Brumidi, a senator said, "The walls of this Capitol will hold his fame fresh and ever increasing as long as they themselves shall stand."

Fiorello La Guardia worked at Ellis Island as an interpreter while he attended law school. La Guardia was deeply touched by the misery he witnessed. He wrote:

One case haunted me for years. A young girl in her teens...was sent to the hospital for observation. I could imagine the effect on this girl, who had always been carefully sheltered and had never been permitted to be in the company of a man alone, when a doctor suddenly rapped on her knees, looked into her eyes, turned her on her back and tickled her spine to ascertain her reflexes. The child rebelled—and how!

Joseph Stella, an Italian immigrant who won fame as an artist in the United States, made this sketch of a husband and wife at Ellis Island in 1905.

ISOLA DELLA LACRIME

Totonno Pappatore, who arrived in New York on May 15, 1906, after a two-week sea voyage, recorded his first impressions in his diary.

By straining our eyes, we could distinguish a thin thread of land on the horizon. In a few hours a string of communities and farms could clearly be seen spread along the coast in one continuous line of habitation. We caught our first glimpse of the Statue of Liberty when, at five o'clock, the ship entered the bay....

The Public Health officials briskly came aboard, and we passed before them like sheep. With the inspection at an end...all of us crowded along the railing to watch the constant traffic of ships, barges, and ferryboats....

It was announced that we would be debarking early in the morning, so we tried to get some sleep. But our excitement and the noise and frenzy of activity on board made sleep impossible. Shortly after midnight we arose to join the others in preparation. At dawn everyone assembled on deck. I was given a number—224—and at eight o'clock we left the ship. It was the beginning of a very long day of utter confusion. We stood around waiting for something to happen. Nothing did. At sunset we were directed aboard ship to spend the night. I thought I had seen the last of that damn compartment, and here I am again, cramped in my little bunk and totally exhausted, with pains down to my toenails. I slept badly and was only too happy to heed the early morning call.

Filing off again, this time we were stuffed into two barges, which were standing nearby. Our barge moved slowly across to Ellis Island and moored on the ferry slip, where we waited for our numbers to be called. Finally, at two o'clock my turn came to leave the barge and go through customs. The customs house is a magnificent building. Once inside, I climbed a long, wide staircase to a huge hall where there were many officials and an even larger number of immigrants. Benches and desks filled the hall and a balcony ran all the way around. Pushed here, pushed there. Get in this line; no, that line; get in that line; no, over there, rush over there, and wait. After answering a few questions, I was given a ticket. Show that ticket to everyone you see, they said. I did. Holding my ticket in front of me, I walked and walked down long, narrow hallways until I arrived at a small room where my eyes were examined. Some people were not passed through, but I was released and continued on always with my ticket showing. Ascending a small staircase, I reached a desk where I had to declare my money. I came here

to make money, but you first have to have money to get into America. I showed the man the three *napoleoni* coins I had borrowed, and he allowed me to proceed.

Another set of stairs took me outside where I passed through more gates, turning left then right then left then right, until I found myself in a large, crowded room divided by a steel fence, which ran up to a high ceiling. The newcomers were on one side like birds in a cage and on the other, with their noses pressed up against the wire, were those persons waiting [for us]. I went from one face to the next. The faces looked at me and I looked at them. Finally, with great relief, I recognized the face of my *compare*, Turiangelo. He is the one responsible for me, and his name is on my declaration of entry. De Carlo, who arrived last week, was with him. They had been there for three days waiting for me to come out. And they had not eaten since the day before. Turiangelo showed the gatekeeper his ticket, and I was given permission to pass through.

Gaetano Conte, an Italian Protestant clergyman, observed Italian immigrants debarking from a ship at Castle Garden in 1890.

I t was a variegated, pathetic, fretful group that descended from the ship: men, women, and children, all of them wearing the unhealthy pallor of steerage passengers. One cried, another laughed, while still another prayed and yet another swore....

The immigrants were queued for the medical inspection. "We don't want to harm you," the doctor assured each nervous and timid Italian while he carried out his examination, fo-

The Great Hall at Ellis Island, which some likened to a cattle pen. Wearing their identification tags on coats or dresses, immigrants wait to be called for the next stage of the examination.

An Italian woman and her child sit outside the detention pen at Ellis Island in 1905. They may be waiting for a relative inside the pen. If one family member was rejected, the others faced the agonizing decision of whether or not to return to Italy with him or her.

Three young Italian brothers standing outside the main building on Ellis Island. Among the papers held by the boy at right is a picture of a saint.

cusing particularly on the head and eyes. Each immigrant anxiously awaited the decision of the doctor, a decision that would either allow him to advance one step closer to the coveted prize, America, or push him thousands of miles back to his village of origin.

Then came the exam before the government inspector. The immigrants were separated into six lines, each line formed inside a fenced enclosure. As each immigrant stood before the inspector's desk, he responded to several questions. How old are you? Are you married? Where does your family live? How much money do you have? Who is waiting for you? What is your job skill? Are you certain you will find employment? Have you been in America previously? Can you read?

How many illusions were shattered by those questions! How many tears were shed! Delinquents, immoral persons, potential beggars, contract workers, the elderly and infirm, women with illegitimate children, returning immigrants who came to work for a short period only (birds of passage): these people are not welcome in America. The inspector would direct Italian phrases to the frightened and defensive immigrant: "Avete monito? Avete monito?" [Do you have any money?] The Italian does not know what to say. Is it better to have or not have money? He does not know so he mumbles something, says nothing, or contradicts himself....

One unkempt woman, with a babe in arms and two little ones clinging to her skirts, was asked by the inspector whether she had an address to go to.... Not understanding what was being asked, she replied: "Yes, sir," and showed him her money and her vaccination certificate. The inspector became increasingly irritated as he continued to repeat himself and she attempted to push the money into his hand. Finally, she was put into detention, sobbing uncontrollably. I saw her the next day and resolved the matter.

A young Sicilian widow, Rita Alfano, arrived at Ellis Island in 1905 with her five-year-old daughter. But her sister-in-law, her sponsor, did not show up. Alfano could not leave until someone vouched for her, and she was detained on the island. She wrote a cry for help to her relatives in Rochester.

I have spent every day and night crying, racking my brain hopelessly trying to find a way of escaping this hell.....What if they send me back to Italy? Oh God, what should I do? I am here desperate with poor Fortunata who keeps on crying and asking when we can leave this place...My dearest sister-in-law, I beg you in the name of God to send your husband as soon as possible because I can't stay here any longer. Please do not forget your unfortunate sister-in-law who has had so many troubles in her life and is now in trouble again.

The letter brought the relatives, and Rita Alfano was released from Ellis Island.

In 1913, Angelo Pellegrini and his family arrived in New York Harbor. The experience at Ellis Island was a "nightmare," but an amazing treat awaited them as well.

At long last we had arrived in America!... We debarked, of course, at Ellis Island, though we then knew nothing about it, nor about its purpose, nor about the annoying routine to which all aliens who entered America had to submit. Had we known, the experience would certainly have been less terrifying. I remember only interminable, uncertain waiting, complete bewilderment. And the horrible rumors!...Why were we herded into those barren rooms? Why were we not taken to the trains so that we might proceed to our several destinations? There was a variety of answers. Someone said that a terrible disease had been discovered among the passengers, and that no one would be permitted to land. Someone else suggested that America was filled up, and that there was no room for anyone who sought employment. An interpreter finally told us that everyone would have to submit to a rigorous eye examination; to which information some starry-eyed optimist added a footnote to the effect that in a large family someone was certain to be rejected.

Well! The Pellegrinis were not rejected. [After obtaining train tickets, they went to a restaurant.] When we sat down in that restaurant, after three weeks of uncertain lunging and heaving in the terrifying Atlantic...every one of us looked shrunken and moth-eaten.... Our stomachs were writhing and squirming in outraged impatience for something good and solid to digest. In brief: we were very hungry. ·

And this is what we were served: sliced oranges, ham, eggs, fried potatoes, buttered toast, coffee, cream, sugar. And then more buttered toast, more coffee, more cream, more sugar. And would we have more toast? Just ask for it. Would we have more coffee, more cream? Just ask for them. As much as we could eat of anything. All for one price. *Just ask for it!* So that was America! Just ask for it! Or, *just reach for it!* For there were the cream and sugar on the table. We had hoped for much from the New World. But we had not hoped for all that. We wondered whether we were not being malignantly deceived.... For our first meal in America—the simple breakfast—we were served all these luxuries! Was that really the meaning of America? Would there be bitter disillusionment later? we wondered as we boarded the train and headed toward the lost horizon.

Fiorello La Guardia

Fiorello La Guardia was born on December 11, 1882, in New York. His father was an immigrant from Foggia, Italy, and his mother came from Trieste. As a band conductor for the U.S. Army, Fiorello's father traveled throughout the country, and Fiorello spent much of his childhood in Arizona.

As a young man, Fiorello went to Europe and served as a filing clerk at the American consulate in Budapest. He used his extra time to study foreign languages, mastering Italian, German, French, and Yiddish. (The skill came in handy when he ran for office because he could speak to New York's many immigrants in their own languages.)

After returning to New York, La Guardia graduated from law school. As a lawyer, he represented the emerging labor unions and soon entered politics. Despite the opposition of New York City's corrupt political machine, he won a seat in Congress in 1916. He spoke out for workers' rights, a minimum wage and a limit on working hours, and elimination of child labor. In these causes he was far ahead of his time. In 1924, he fought against the law restricting immigration, calling it the result of racial prejudice.

But it was as mayor of New York that La Guardia made his mark. Serving for three terms from 1934 to 1945, he was known affectionately as "Little Flower," the translation of his first name. The five-foot, three-inch La Guardia was always at the heart of the action, riding to fires on fire engines and personally smashing the gambling machines that his government declared illegal.

In a city where corruption in government had been the rule, he had a strong reputation for honesty. He read all his mail and went out into the city to see for himself the results of his policies. To get things done, he worked 16-hour days. During a newspaper strike, he took time off from his duties to read the comics to children over the radio.

After retiring from the mayor's office on New Year's Day 1946, he worked for the relief of wartime refugees. When he died in 1947, all city flags flew at half-mast in his honor. He is regarded today as the best mayor that the nation's largest city has ever had.

For some people their first experience in America was a disappointment. One immigrant remembered, "New York was awful. The streets were full of horse manure. My town in Italy, Avelino, was much more beautiful. I said to myself; 'How come, America?' On hot days when the manure dried, the wind lifted it into the air like confetti and breathing became difficult."

Years later another immigrant laughed at his own naïveté. When he first arrived, he saw a group of Italians digging in the street and looked forward to trying his luck at finding the gold underneath the pavement. "In the old country they used to say that America was a rich and wonderful place—so rich you could pick gold up in the street. And I believed it!"

On arrival in New York City, Vittorio Buttis had his picture taken and printed onto a postcard to send to a friend in Rutland, Vermont. Many immigrants found work in the stone quarries in Vermont.

FINDING A PAESANO

Often immigrants were greeted by paesani, *people they knew from the old country who were willing to take them in and find jobs for them. But a* paesano *(or paesana) could be anyone who looked Italian, for the language barrier was the single greatest obstacle that the newcomers had to overcome.*

When Elizabeth Marrelli was nearly 100 years old, she remembered how a paesano *helped her find the man who had wooed her by mail.*

When I was nineteen, I received letters from America. They were written by a gentleman named Francisco Felice [who lived in a town called Helper, Utah].... Frank's letters and my responses were read and written by my aunt who was the village interpreter. After two years of corresponding, Frank sent me the money to go to America and become his wife.

I left my village, wearing a sign saying Salt Lake City, Utah....When I arrived in New York City, I was stranded for three days because I was thirty-five dollars short for my train fare....

I had neither food nor money and I was only able to say, "Helper, Utah, America" in English, so I sat on the hard wooden bench alone in the big train depot. Finally, a shopkeeper close by the depot came to help me. He was Italian and was able to speak with me. He wired Frank Felice in Helper, Utah, and was able to get me the money....

My long journey finally ended at Salt Lake City, Utah. There I met Francisco Felice. He was a very handsome man.

In his autobiography, Pascal D'Angelo gives a vivid description of his first impressions as he left Ellis Island on April 20, 1910. He and his father had been met by a man they knew from their native village, who had found work for the new arrivals.

Mario Lancia, our new foreman, met us at the Battery. He shook hands with all of us and remarked on my having grown into a broad, husky lad. I grinned and turned, startled at the sight of an elevated train dashing around the curve towards South Ferry. To my surprise, not even one car fell. Nor did the people walking beneath scurry away at its approach as I would have done.

Chattering happily, we started to cross a broad street. All at once there was a terrific crash overhead.... [Lancia], smiling, explained the roar to me. "It's only the train over us."

I felt as if those unseen wheels above were grinding paths

through my own body. [They entered the elevated railway car.] We sat down. A most inconceivable vision was flashing past the car window. As we traveled on, and my dazed eyes became accustomed to the place, I began to look around. A matronly lady sitting opposite was scanning me with a sort of pitying gaze. I wondered whether I should get up and bow to her. Then I noticed that right next to the lady sat a father and son. Upright and straight, they were both glaring at a newspaper which the father held. With compassion, I observed that they were both afflicted with some nervous disease, for their mouths were in continuous motion, like cows chewing cud. "Too bad," I thought, "that both father and son should be afflicted in the same way!" [This was D'Angelo's first sight of a person chewing gum.]

The foreman was anxious, pulling out a watch continually and saying that we had barely time to catch a train for our final destination. So we were not to live in this remarkable place! And now, just before we reached the station, I began to notice that there were signs at the corners of the streets with "Ave.! Ave.! Ave.!" How religious a place this must be that expresses its devotion at every crossing, I mused. Still, they did not put the "Ave." before the holy word, as, in "Ave Maria," but rather after. How topsy-turvy!

Attilio Piccirilli came to the United States from Tuscany in 1888, when he was 22. He became a famous sculptor, designing monuments in New York City and Washington, D.C. At the age of 74, he recalled his first sight of America.

My brother and I first came over here together.... We were boys, with big eyes—boys leaning over the boat rail watching New York harbor. I had 25 cents in my pocket. I remember, and my brother and I discussed whether, if our uncle didn't meet us that day, it would be enough to buy some bread and cheese.

There's one big difference right there. Today we wouldn't be allowed to land in America with 25 cents in our pockets! They were glad to have us come in those days for there weren't enough Americans to do the work over here.... My uncle *was* there to meet us with a friend. Right away they led us off to show us all of the sights....

Everyone had a clean shirt and a shaved face, and I asked my uncle, "What day is today?" "Tuesday," he told me.

"No. No," I said. "I mean what fete [feast] day is it! Everybody is washed and wearing white shirts—it must be a great national holiday."

My uncle and his friend laughed. "Oh," they told us, "it isn't a fete day. People wear clean shirts every day in America." I was more impressed by that than anything they showed me. Two days later I took out my first citizenship papers, and I think that I have been a good American ever since.

Arriving in Lamerica could be confusing. Bartolomeo Vanzetti described his initial reaction:

Until yesterday I was among folks who understood me. This morning I seemed to have awakened in a land where my language meant little more to the native (as far as meaning was concerned) than the pitiful noises of a dumb animal. Where was I to go? What was I to do? Here was the promised land. The elevated rattled by and did not answer. The automobiles and trolley sped by, heedless of me.

Frequently, husbands went to the New World first and sent for their families after they found jobs and homes. In 1911, the St. Raphael's Italian Benevolent Society helped this group of immigrants to find transportation to relatives on the West Coast.

At immigrant landing stations such as Castle Garden and Ellis Island, newcomers could buy railroad tickets to their destinations inland. Some were worried by the fact that their baggage traveled in a separate car, but if they held onto the baggage checks, they (usually) found it at the end of the journey.

Italian laborers accepted construction work that was often dangerous. These men, photographed in 1910, are driving a tunnel, probably for a subway line. New York's rapid transit system, the largest in the nation, was built between 1900 and the mid-1930s.

CHAPTER FOUR

GOING TO WORK

An Italian immigrant is said to have remarked, "I came to America because I heard the streets were paved with gold. When I got here, I found out three things: first, the streets weren't paved with gold; second, they weren't paved at all; and third, I was expected to pave them." And pave them he did, for the overwhelming reason that Italians came to the United States was to find work.

Italians who arrived before 1870 were often skilled artisans. In 1622, a group of glassblowers from Venice arrived in the Jamestown colony. A century and a half later, Thomas Jefferson, inspired by classical structures he had seen while visiting Italy, designed his great house, Monticello. He brought Italian stoneworkers to turn his plans into reality.

Highly skilled workers and artists, such as Da Ponte and Brumidi, did not come in great numbers. By the mid-18th century, only a few thousand Italians had arrived in the United States. In the 1850 census, the state with the largest Italian American population was Louisiana, where the Italians earned a living as fishermen and small farmers. The 1849 Gold Rush brought a surge of Italian prospectors to the

West Coast, and by 1860 California claimed more Italian Americans (2,805) than any other state. Some stayed on to plant orchards and vineyards in the sunny climate that was so like the one they had left in Italy.

The events of the Risorgimento before 1861 brought political exiles like Garibaldi, who lived for a time in Staten Island. During the U.S. Civil War, a group of patriotic Italians in New York formed the "Garibaldi Guard" to fight on the Union side. They carried into battle, along with the American flag, the banner of Garibaldi's Redshirts, on which was written Mazzini's motto: "God and the People." The Confederacy also had its share of Italian soldiers, most of whom fought in a unit organized in New Orleans, called the Italian Guards.

Most of those in the great wave of Italian immigrants that began arriving in the 1870s were sojourners. They intended to find jobs, save a nest egg, and return to the old country. Though a few Italians formed farming communities, the great majority took work they described as "pickashovel."

Between 1870 and 1920, the United States was thriving and expanding. New railroads and roads were needed to bring goods from one part of the country to another.

Growing cities required new streets and buildings. Production from mines and factories increased. The desperately poor Italian immigrants, ready to take any job they could get, provided a willing work force, laying down railroad tracks, building streets and subways, hacking stone from quarries, working long hours in factories.

Their greatest task was the construction of the great city in which they first arrived. From 1880 to 1930, New York was the nation's fastest-growing urban center. In the words of one city official in 1890, "We can't get along without Italians. We want someone to do the dirty work." Italians helped to construct New York's skyscrapers, bridges, tunnels, subways, and streets.

Other Italians were lured outside the city to work in railroad gangs, quarries, mines, and construction. Very often, the newcomers were met at the boat by a *padrone* (boss), a fellow Italian who was paid to hire workers for specific projects and send them to the work site. Placed aboard a train or horse-drawn wagon, the newcomers soon found themselves delivered into the hands of another tough padrone who would direct them, pay their meager wages, and ensure that they worked hard. Some padroni were even sent to

Italy to recruit laborers and arrange for their passage to the United States.

Though the padrone system helped the newcomers to find jobs, it also exploited them. Padroni were earlier immigrants who sometimes took advantage of those who followed. The padrone's chief weapon was that he knew the English language, which most new arrivals did not. The Italians could not complain to any other authority when the padrone charged so much for food and other necessities that virtually nothing was left of the workers' wages.

Seeking the company of their *compari* —other Italians—the immigrants congregated in their own neighborhoods in the large cities. In order to survive, all members of the family went to work. Children sold newspapers and shined shoes. Men accepted any type of labor they could find. Some sold goods from pushcarts, hawking their wares throughout the immigrant neighborhoods. The traveling Italian organ grinder, playing music on a portable machine, became a familiar sight. Women went to work in clothing factories, often taking home piecework so they could watch their children while sewing garments for which they were paid "by the piece." Frequently, the children and the men joined in the piecework, laboring far into the night to make additional money for the family.

The wages the Italians earned were shockingly low. A report by the U.S. Immigration Commission in 1910 showed that the average Italian-born male earned only $396 a year. By contrast, the national average was $666. Italians were at the bottom of the ladder, below African Americans, who earned an average of $445 in 1910. And yet many Italian Americans still thought themselves better off than they had been in Italy. Some called America the land of *dolci dollari*— "sweet money."

Italians, like most other immigrants, found themselves the objects of prejudice and discrimination. Even those who never learned English knew that the terms *wop*

Carmen Giorgio worked in Philadelphia in the 1920s. He delivered blocks of ice that people used in home iceboxes to preserve food.

and *dago* were fighting words. *Wop* supposedly came from the phrase "without passport" that immigration officials stamped on the entry papers of those who fled Italy without bothering to apply for official permission. The origin of *dago* is less certain. Some scholars think it originally applied to Italians who were hired for a day's labor— "day-go."

Second-generation Italian Americans were particularly hurt by such prejudice, for they looked at their parents through the eyes of Americans. Young Fiorello La Guardia, living at an Arizona army

post where his father was stationed, was humiliated when an Italian organ grinder arrived. La Guardia never forgot the taunts of the other children who reminded him that he and the organ grinder were both "dagos." Years later, when Fiorello became the first Italian American mayor of New York, he banned organ grinders from the city's streets.

Name-calling was not the worst of the treatment Italian Americans endured. In 1891, after nine Sicilians in New Orleans were acquitted by a jury of the charge of murder, a mob stormed the jail. Eleven Italians were dragged outside and lynched. It was not the last time that Italians would suffer such a fate. Newspapers and politicians fanned the flames of bigotry against them.

Yet Italians fought back, remembering that they were the heirs to a great cultural and intellectual tradition. Italian Americans were among the leaders of labor unions who fought for better wages and working conditions. Indeed, the Italian Americans were often among the most radical labor leaders, active in such organizations as the Industrial Workers of the World (IWW). A small number of Italian immigrants were anarchists—those who opposed any kind of organized government. This too was a carryover from Europe, where anarchist movements were more powerful than in the United States.

Italian Americans led strikes by mineworkers in the western states, by silkworkers in New Jersey, and by textile workers in New England.

The 1912 struggle between workers and factory owners in Lawrence, Massachusetts, became a legendary turning point in the union movement in the United States. When the police and state militia clubbed women and children trying to leave the city, the sympathy of the nation was aroused. Congress held an investigation, and in time passed laws that protected workers from the exploitation that the strikers had fought.

Many industrious Italian Americans, of course, moved up from padrone labor, pushcarts, and piecework. They opened their own businesses, such as grocery stores and restaurants in immigrant neighborhoods.

Some of these entrepreneurs became American success stories. After going to Scranton, Pennsylvania, Amadeo Obici worked at his uncle's fruit stand. Picking up English and saving his money, in 1897 Obici decided to go into business for himself. He rented sidewalk space and sold roasted peanuts. Soon he packed his product in paper bags, selling them for a nickel apiece. Obici had a sense of marketing, and in each bag he placed a coupon with a letter from his name. A customer who collected coupons spelling the full name received a dollar pocket watch. This was the beginning of the Planters Peanut Company. Obici's symbol, Mr. Peanut, became a nationally recognized trademark. It came from a drawing contest that Obici

sponsored for local schoolchildren. He took the winner, a peanut shell with a head and legs, and added the top hat, spats, and cane.

Even more famous is Hector Boiardi, who helped to make spaghetti one of America's favorite foods. Working as a chef after he came to America around 1915, he moved from hotel to hotel. His reputation grew when he catered President Woodrow Wilson's wedding reception. After opening his own restaurant in Cleveland, Boiardi found that patrons liked the food so much they wanted

A fisherman repairing nets in San Francisco around 1905. The Italian community in the city's North Beach section included many Sicilians who had earned their living from the sea in the old country and continued to do so in America.

portions to take home. He started a company to produce sauce and spaghetti in cans. Because even his own sales force found it difficult to pronounce his name, he labeled the product phonetically: Chef Boy-Ar-Dee.

Italian Americans found their greatest early successes on the West Coast, where they planted orchards and vineyards that led to fruit-shipping companies and wineries. The Italian Swiss Colony vineyard at Asti, California, celebrated the construction of a new concrete wine tank in 1897 by holding a dance for 200 people—

inside the tank. Italian family names such as Gallo, Petri, and Sebastiani appear on the labels of today's California wines. The Di Giorgio Fruit Company, founded by two brothers from Sicily, became the largest shipper of fresh fruit in the world, under the S & W label. In 1889, Marco Fontana, an immigrant from Genoa, started the California Fruit Packing Corporation, which put the now-familiar name Del Monte on its products.

The greatest Italian American success story in California began with Amadeo Pietro Giannini, the son of Italian immigrants. Giannini founded a storefront bank in San Francisco's North Beach, the Italian section of the city, in 1904. Catering to the residents of the area, he called his little establishment the Bank of Italy. Giannini lent money to people based on his judgment of their character. Frank Capra, who would later become a legendary film director, remembered that Giannini lent money to a friend of his father to build a spaghetti-sauce factory—just because Giannini liked the taste of the sauce. The small bank prospered under such policies, and in 1928, it was renamed the Bank of America. Giannini lived long enough to see it become the largest bank in the United States. Today, its headquarters, the TransAmerica Building, towers over San Francisco. It is a symbol of the success of the Italians who came to the United States looking for jobs and willing to work hard.

PICK AND SHOVEL

The padrones, *or Italian work agents, often preyed on newcomers at Ellis Island and other entry ports. Taking advantage of the fact that most of the immigrants could not speak English, the padrones obtained jobs for them—but at a high price, sometimes 60 percent of their wages. Rocco Corresca described how he and another boy were recruited by a padrone at Ellis Island. Because Rocco and his friend had no money, the immigration officials were about to return them to Italy.*

B ut a man named Bartolo came up and told them that we were brothers and he was our uncle and would take care of us. He brought two other men who swore that they knew us in Italy and that Bartolo was our uncle. I had never seen any of them before, but even then Bartolo might be my uncle, so I did not say anything. The bosses of the island let us go out with Bartolo....

We came to Brooklyn, New York, to a wooden house in Adams Street that was full of Italians from Naples. Bartolo had a room on the third floor and there were fifteen men in the room, all boarding with Bartolo....

The next morning, early, Bartolo told us to go out and pick rags and get bottles. He gave us bags and hooks and showed us the ash barrels. On the streets where the fine houses are, the people are very careless and put out good things, like mattresses and umbrellas, clothes, hats, and boots. We brought all these to Bartolo, and he made them new again and sold them on the sidewalk. But mostly we brought rags and bones. The rags we had to wash in the back yard and then we hung them to dry on lines under the ceiling in our room. The bones we kept under the beds till Bartolo could find a man to buy them.

Most of the men in our room worked at digging the sewer. Bartolo got them the work and they paid him about one quarter of their wages. Then he charged them for board and he bought the clothes for them, too. So they got little money after all. Bartolo was always saying that the rent of the room was so high that he could not make anything, but he was really making plenty. He was what they call a *padrone* and is now a very rich man. The men that were living with him had just come to America and could not speak English—Bartolo told us all that we must work for him and that if we did not the police would come and put us in prison....

We were with Bartolo nearly a year, but some of our countrymen who had been in the place a long time said that Bartolo had no right to us and we could get work for a dollar and a half a day, which, when you make it *lire* (Italian currency), is very much. So we went away one day to Newark and got work

Immigrant laborers working on the Cleveland Belt Line Railroad around 1910. More than 2 million Italians arrived in the United States between 1901 and 1910, and this was typical of the kind of work they found.

on the street. Bartolo came after us and made a great noise, but the boss said that if he did not go away soon the police would have him. Then he went, saying that there was no justice in this country....

[Rocco and Francesco worked at a series of jobs, saving their money.] We went back to Brooklyn to a saloon near Hamilton Ferry where we got a job cleaning it out and slept in a little room upstairs. There was a bootblack named Michael on the corner and when I had time I helped him and learned the business. Francesco cooked the lunch in the saloon and he, too, worked for the bootblack and we were soon able to make the best polish.

Then we thought we would go into business and we got a basement on Hamilton Avenue, near the Ferry, and put four chairs in it.... We had tables and looking glasses there and curtains.... Outside we had a big sign that said:

THE BEST SHINE FOR TEN CENTS

Men that did not want to pay 10 cents could get a good shine for 5 cents but it was not an oil shine. We had two boys helping us and paid each of them 50 cents a day. The rent of the place was $20 a month, so the expenses were very great, but we made money from the beginning....

We had said that when we saved $1,000 each we would go back to Italy and buy a farm, but now that the time is coming we are so busy and making so much money that we think we will stay.

"Pick and shovel" jobs were easy to find. The growing cities of the United States needed transportation systems, sewage and water pipelines, buildings, bridges, and roads. This group is constructing a reservoir on the Schuylkill River to provide fresh water to Philadelphia, around 1898.

A 15-year-old Italian immigrant described how a padrone in Ohio hired him to work on a railroad gang.

The boss said that if I wanted to work I would have to come to him, because Americans wouldn't hire any Italian except through him. I didn't want to sign up for four months' work.... But my money was nearly gone. So I finally put my name down. The *padrone* wanted $6 *bossatura* [the fee for the boss], but as I had only $3 left, he took that and agreed to have the railroad company give him the other three out of my first pay envelope....

[The workers lived in railroad cars.] As I entered one car for the first time, the odor choked me. I saw eight beds of boards placed across two boxes. On these lay bags of straw, and for a covering the men used old tan coats or horse blankets. The blankets were covered with vermin. Dirt of two years covered the mattresses....

Sharply at five o'clock the boss leaped from his car and began cursing at the men. The poor laborers trembled and hurried. In a moment five hand cars were on the rails. After riding six miles, we arrived at our destination. Amid more cursing the men took the cars off the track and began to tear up the old rails. In a few seconds the sweat was rolling in streams. The rails were heavy and the men worked with might and main all morning. There was no let-up, no mercy. From shortly after five until noon, about seven hours, the men labored without rest. "The beasts," said the *padrone*, "must not be given a rest, otherwise they will step over me."... With nothing but coffee in the morning and bread at noon, these men worked for ten hours every day under the blistering sun or in pouring rain. Stopping work at four, the men returned to their ramshackle cars to cook, eat, and sleep.

Sometimes the immigrants right off the boat were tricked into signing up for work gangs. One recalled:

We started from New York on November 3, 1891, under the guidance of two bosses. We had been told we should go to Connecticut to work on a railroad and earn one dollar and seventy-five cents per day. We were taken instead to South Carolina, first to a place called Lambs and then after a month or so to the "Tom Tom" sulfate mines. The railroad fare was eight dollars and eighty-five cents; this sum, as well as the price of our tools, nearly three dollars, we owed the bosses. We were received by an armed guard, which kept constant watch over us, accompanying us every morning from the barracks to the mines and at night again from the work to our shanty.... Part of our pay went toward the extinction of our debt; the rest was spent at the "pluck-me" store. We got only so much as would keep us from starvation. Things cost us more than twice or three times their regular price. Our daily fare was coffee and bread for breakfast, rice with lard or soup at dinner-time, and cheese and sausage for supper. Yet we were not able to pay off our debt; so after a while we were given only bread, and with this only to sustain us we had to go through our daily work. By and by we became exhausted, and some of us got sick. Then we decided to try, at the risk of our lives, to escape. Some of us ran away, eluding the guards. After a run of an hour I was exhausted and decided to stay for the night in the woods. We were, however, soon surprised by the appearance of the bosses and two guards. They thrust guns in our faces and ordered us to return to work or they would shoot us down. We answered that we would rather die than resume our former life in the mine. The bosses then sent for two black policemen, who insisted that we should follow them. We went before a judge, who was sitting in a bar-room. The judge asked if there was any written contract, and when he heard there wasn't, said he would let us go free. But the bosses, the policemen, and the judge then held a short consultation, and the result was that the bosses paid some money (I believe it was forty-five dollars), the policemen put the manacles on our wrists, and we were marched off. At last on April 1, we were dismissed on account of the hot weather.... I had only one dollar and with this, not knowing either the country or the language, I had to walk to New York. After forty-two days I arrived in the city utterly exhausted.

The padrone system was informal and some immigrants worked their way into it by learning English. One former padrone told his story to the Ethnic Survey of the Federal Writer's Project during the Great Depression. He was born in 1872, in the small village of Oratina and came to the United States as a 15-year-old boy. He worked on the Erie Railroad in Newark, New Jersey. He picked up English and on his 18th birthday learned that he had been advanced to foreman. This brought about a change in his life.

During the course of our working day, there were many occasions for various men to call on me in reference to work, and they would almost always address me as padrone. It got so that in about a year, I really was "padrone this" and "padrone that." Without realizing it fully, I had acquired a moniker which carried more meaning than I realized at the time. Before I fully appreciated it, I became quite a leader among our entire Italian group, for so many had come to me for employment....

So one day I realized I could be happily married on my present salary, which was about fifteen dollars per week; so I expressed my thoughts one evening at a local gathering saloon to my numerous friends, more or less in a joking way, but I didn't do anything about it. But my friends did, for in about a month's time I had received several photographs of girls in my hometown and other towns adjoining; so that I was not long in selecting one which appealed to me, and arrangements were made immediately by her brother, a friend and an employee in my crew. Soon after, his sister arrived at Ellis Island. We both went over to receive her, and I lost no time in getting married, for I had prepared a home for us all—a six-room cold flat—

"Breaker boys" in a Pennsylvania coal mine in 1911. Those under age 12 were supposed to work above ground, but many lied about their ages, for the pay was better for those below. They earned between $1 and $3 a week.

A West Virginia miner after his workday had ended. Even in 1938, when this photo was taken, mining companies provided only the bare necessities for their workers.

with an understanding that her brother was to board with us. That day and several days after were spent in celebrating our marriage, and almost everyone came to see us and bring these various gifts of money and good wishes.

Well, not long after that, everyone wanted to board with us. So I bought beds, and I furnished, at one time, bed and board for about twenty-four men. I also furnished, at extra cost, their wine for their meals. Well, conditions being what they are, most of my countrymen soon were entrusting to my care all of their savings and not expecting any interest in return. I, in turn, invested in real estate and deposited in various banks all of their savings and mine, too. Besides this, from time to time, I would furnish in part, or all, necessary expenses for many countrymen to come to America; and then, on arrival, I would put them up at my place, which by this time had become a center of activities, and also provided jobs for them, so that eventually they would repay me for all the money I had advanced them, at figures which I quoted, with no questions asked by anyone. I enjoyed their faith so, that I was respected as a father in general, and I also arranged and promoted a number of matrimonies. I selected and bought all necessary furnishings for such an occasion. Then, too, as time went on, some of my boarders having saved quite a lot of money, I would induce them to buy a small home, which I would sell them, for I had acquired six or seven or eight of them....

This condition prevailed for quite a long time, till I decided that I should own a saloon for the betterment of everyone concerned and for a greater financial income for me. In due time, I secured a license and opened a saloon in one of my properties. Later, I also established a grocery store, in which I sold Italian and American merchandise, rounding out a means of supply of foodstuffs and other wants for my employees, friends, and boarders. During all these years, no one ever regarded me as anything but a benefactor; and to this day, I enjoy all of my friends' respect. My counsel and advice are sought by them, wherever they feel they need it.

Constantine Panunzio arrived in Boston in 1902. He and a French sailor, named Louis, found lodging in a boardinghouse in the North End, the Italian section of Boston.

It was a "three-room apartment" and the landlady informed us that she was already "full," but since we had no place to go, she would take us in. Added to the host [of people] that was already gathered there, our coming made fourteen people. At night the floor of the kitchen and the dining table were turned into beds. Louis and I were put to sleep in one of the beds with two other men, two facing north and two south....

We began to make inquiries about jobs and were promptly informed that there was plenty of work at "pick and shovel." We were also given to understand by our fellow-boarders that "pick and shovel" was practically the only work available to Italians. Now these were the first two English words I had

Italian laborers working on New York City's Sixth Avenue Elevated Railway in 1910. Typically, they earned $1.75 a day. "All those bridges, all those roads, all those railroads—they were all built by people who worked hard," wrote the son of one Italian immigrant.

heard and they possessed great charm. Moreover, if I were to earn money to return home and this was the only work available for Italians, they were very weighty words for me, and I must master them as soon and as well as possible and then set out to find their hidden meaning. I practiced for a day or two until I could say "peek" and "shuvle" to perfection. Then I asked a fellow-boarder to take me to see what the work was like. He did. He led me to Washington Street, not far from the colony, where some excavation work was going on, and there I did see, with my own eyes, what the "peek" and "shuvle" were about. My heart sank within me, for I had thought it some form of office work; but I was game and since this was the only work available for Italians, and since I must have money to return home, I would take it up.

In 1902, Angelo Massari journeyed to Tampa, Florida, where his cousin lived.

I n those days there was nothing else to do in Tampa but make cigars, and all immigrants...landed in the cigar factories. I was one of them.... At the end of May...I was presented with an envelope containing $5.60 as payment for half of my work. That day was a happy one for me...the day when I could support myself and cease to be a burden on my cousin's shoulders had finally arrived....

That very week my cousin Giambattista was married, and while I badly needed the first fruits of my toil, I said to my new cousin Maria, "I have nothing to offer you, and you know that these are the first dollars that I have ever earned. I am really sorry that they are few, and that I cannot do better." Then I gave my new cousin the little envelope with my first earnings. I was left without a penny, but I was not worried, for the coming week I was going to get the same amount of money and maybe more....

In the factory we had four hours of reading every day. The reader would stand on a high platform in the center of the *galeras* and read in Castilian [Spanish, the native language of many of the factory workers] for a solid hour the news of the day, then we listened for three hours to interesting feature articles and novels of well-known writers.... The reader used to submit a list of books that were available, and the cigarmakers took a vote. The book accepted by the majority of the workers was placed on the lectern.

The reader was paid by the cigarmakers. A good reader got twenty-five cents from each worker.... I enjoyed the reading, paying the greatest attention to the reader. As a matter of fact, when I left the factory, the only thing that I missed was the reading, not the twenty-four dollars a week that I was earning. The factory was like a popular university, teaching the workers many things that they had never known.

A hearty lunch, with some wine to wash it down, sustained the Italian workers.

WORKING THE LAND

Italians established a number of farming colonies in different parts of the United States. One of the most famous, at Vineland, New Jersey, was started by Secchi de Casale, a follower of Garibaldi. De Casale had fled Italy in 1849 after Garibaldi failed to establish a republic in Rome. De Casale started the first Italian newspaper in New York, called L'Eco d'Italia. *In 1878, de Casale brought a group of Italian farmers to work on land around Vineland. They planted grapes, sweet potatoes, beans, tomatoes, and peach trees—with such success that a large cannery opened to process their produce.*

Other notable Italian farm communities grew up in St. Helena, North Carolina, and Genoa, Wisconsin. In St. Helena, a local landowner formed a company to sell land on credit and provide tools. Over time Italian farmers could save enough to pay off their debt; then they would own the farm. Felice Ferrero, an Italian journalist, described the process.

The company's contract with the immigrants was made so that to each immigrant it sells a small farm of ten, fifteen, twenty acres....The company builds for the immigrant—and at his expense—a small, but well-constructed bungalow of three rooms, costing $250. It gives him also the implements and animals needed for a successful start. For all this the company requests no payment in advance. If an immigrant begins with ten acres, his debt will be about $600, aside from the money that he may have borrowed for his voyage.

Supplied with a house and...tools, the peasant finds himself face to face with his ten-acre swamp, heavily wooded. Long, weary toil must yet be his before he can get crops from his land....

If he can withstand the dangers and the strain of the first year, however, recompense follows promptly. His land gives him four crops of vegetables annually.... Then the produce is carried to New York by fast trains, in refrigerating cars, and marketed by the expert agents of the company.... Of these returns the company generally keeps one-half, and the other half goes to the farmer. Some farmers have been able to pay off most of their debt and to accumulate a little pile besides, and the life of the colony barely counts four years. What more attractive inducement could be held out to a foreign peasant, whose life has been a miserable *via crucis* through debts and want, than the prospect of becoming within five or six years the independent proprietor of a farm, able to give him an annual income of $1,500 or more?

Italian men and women worked as day laborers at harvest time on the farms of New Jersey, which has a large Italian American population.

Father Pietro Bandini, an Italian priest, went to Arkansas around 1900. He helped to organize a group of Italian immigrants into an agricultural cooperative. Father Bandini purchased about 900 acres of farmland in northwestern Arkansas. The immigrants named their new community Tontitown in memory of Enrico Tonti, an Italian who had explored the region in the 1600s. However, other settlers in the area tried to drive the Italians out. The Italians' church, which had been built with money contributed by Queen Margherita of Italy, was burned to the ground. After the church was rebuilt, an anti-Italian mob torched it a second time. Undaunted, Father Bandini rebuilt it once more. The next time the marauders approached, he stood in front of the church with his parishioners at his side and declared:

We are all Americans here and I give you notice that we shall exercise the American right of self-defense. There are few men among us who have not served in the Italian army. We are familiar with our guns. I am hereafter colonel of our regiment and I assure you that night and day a sentinel shall patrol our streets. Any person coming among us and manifesting malice will be shot.

The mob dispersed and gave Tontitown no further trouble. Today it remains a thriving little town in a region whose farmers raise grapes and other fruit.

In 1904, when Regina Dottavio was four years old, she arrived in the United States with her parents. Seventy-five years later, she told an interviewer what brought them to Vineland, New Jersey.

My parents came to America because they weren't working in Italy. There was no work for them; it was hard to make a living. Somebody came and told us that we ought to come to America, that they would pay our fare. So, we decided to come.

We landed in New Orleans. We lived in the South for about four years....

My father and mother both worked in the cotton fields. They had it hard, too. Because there was a lot of malaria, a lot of sickness. It was hot all of the time, and my father was always sick.

We stayed there four years, I think. Then the fellow who interpreted for us—he spoke English—said, "This is no place for you people. You'll never make any money here." He was from Vineland and offered to take us there....

Interviewer: And when you got here, what type of work did your father do? Farming?

Dottavio: No. He would have done anything. He used to go to the glass factory, and there was no work. Most of the time they'd say, "Come tomorrow, come tomorrow, there's no work." We had it hard.

Then in the summertime, they started work in the fields. My mother and father both worked with a farmer. They only got fifty cents a day.... My folks worked in shares with the boss of the farm and after they got a little money, they bought the farm.

One successsful Italian immigrant community was Vineland, New Jersey, where this bountiful crop of tomatoes grew. The tomato was originally grown by Native Americans in South America and Mexico. Taken to Europe around 1550, it acquired the Italian name pomo d'oro, or "apple of gold." Tomatoes were seldom eaten in the United States until the late 19th century, when Italian immigrants showed how delicious they were.

WOMEN'S WORK

Marie Costa and her children, in a Cincinnati market in 1908, sell baskets they have woven at home.

With her mother and younger sisters, Grace Calabrese arrived from Italy in 1924 when she was 14. Her father, who had been in the United States three years, found a small apartment for his family.

We were here only about a week and my father says to me, "Come on, you have to start traveling with me. I have to show you all the trains. You have to get to work." He needed help. I wasn't supposed to go to work, not even fifteen, but I was the oldest girl....Oh, I was so excited! He put me on the subway and he made me go back and forth two or three times to teach me. I was a little bit afraid, yeah. But, you know, then the next day I went the same way. I didn't even move an inch. And I started to learn a little bit the trains.

I find a job in New York. They used to make keys, locks. I worked about a couple of months. That was one of my first jobs. There was all American people. There was no Italians at all. I didn't know one word English.... [After losing her job, she told her father] "Pop, I know you need help and I'm the oldest girl in the house. I'll go to work, but let me go to an evening school for a couple of hours." They were afraid to send me. They think somebody was going to grab me, things like that.

Like their brothers, girls hawked newspapers on city streets. This Italian newsgirl, wearing a hat and veil, poses proudly in 1896 at the busy corner of Sixth Avenue and 23rd Street in New York City.

So I never went to school here, and until today I am mad at my parents; they didn't make me go to school a little bit.

My grandmother was a dressmaker in Italy, and somehow was in me sewing. I used to love that. I wanted to sew all the time and to get a job that I loved. So then I find, about a couple of months later, there was an ad in the paper, in the Italian, the *Progresso* paper, and I said to my girlfriends, "How about if we try this job?" They telling in the paper, "No experience required, will teach you." In the garment industry in New York, about Thirty-seventh Street I think it was. So we got to New York, the three of us; and being that I used to sew so much, I was pretty good with the electric machine, and in half a day I learned how to run that machine.... [A]fter one week they thought I was pretty bright and they gave me something else to do. I was making the whole garment. I stayed there about two months, and after that I moved on, to the better shops where they made a better garment, like suits and things like that.

The conditions wasn't bad. I came from Europe—I thought it was fine. We had dressing room, bathrooms. For me it was good.... [At the time there was no union in the shop where she worked.] I even went to work on a Sunday, you know, because we wanted to work—we needed the money so bad. I didn't understand then, but afterward we realized that the union was good, because we got a lot of good out of it, you know. We got holidays paid. But before we didn't care. We didn't know any better; let's put it that way. We came from plain people, we didn't know. We just wanted to work and make a few dollars and that was it.

Geraldine Cozza described her mother working in the family's apartment in the 1920s:

My mother took some homework at home, because she didn't want to leave us alone. She would sew, and I used to help her too. We used to sit on the fire escape, in New York City, sewing early in the morning in them hot days. But we were happy to be here because we had more to look forward to than what we had over there.

Josephine Costanzo described her mother working in a mill:

My mother was a twister in the Lawrence mills. It was unusual; in Italy there were no jobs for women. In fact, people that heard about it back in the village didn't like the idea of the women working. But my mother felt she was doing no different from all the women, so she decided she was going to work. Make some money.

The son of a Sicilian immigrant recalled how his whole family worked in their Brooklyn tenement. They assembled lapel pins in the shape of a cross studded with diamonds:

What you had to do was to glue tiny artificial diamonds in the holes on the lapel pin.

After supper my mother would clear the tables, take the glass protectors off the wheels of the furniture, and pour some glue in each glass coaster. It smelled like nail polish remover and gasoline. My kid brother was put to bed, then my father brought the lapel pins and spilled them on the table. They made a huge pile...we'd work until after midnight but never after one. At least I wouldn't for I had to go to school in the morning. Yet sometimes I would hear my mother get up because she couldn't sleep with "thought" in her head. And then my father would holler at her, *"Rimbabita*, you will kill yourself"; and my mother would answer, "Sh-hhh. The children are sleeping."

Women in the garment trade often worked at home, where they could tend their children. Their employers gave them stacks of pre-cut pieces of clothing, which they carried home to sew together. Women in garment factories were usually paid about half of what men earned, but home workers were paid "by the piece."

Immigrant women often went to work in clothing factories. Rosina Giuliani's daughter related how her mother's skill won her a good job.

Mama always knew how to make beautiful hats. When she first came here, they used to tease her in the factory. Rosina, Rosina, you're the fastest in the shop, they used to say. Mama became a forelady because she showed the boss how to make her beautiful hats. He used her skill and made her a forelady. Mama taught Papa how to make hats. They tried to go into business themselves, but failed because they never had enough money to get started. That's why they ended up in the factory for most of their lives.

Work in the clothing factories was hard. Agnes Santucci recalled:

The machine used to go, keep agoing, keep agoing. I was so unhappy to stay there all day, no go out like it was a prison. I couldn't speak English. I used to stay at the machine all day without seeing anybody. The forelady used to be back and forth, back and forth, look this way, look the other way. Do your work, do your work. An Italian girl fell asleep at the machine and she was fired.

And Grace Grimaldi thought her job making blouses was like slavery.

Between the years 1914 and 1928, it was a slavery really. You couldn't open your mouth. God forbid you came five minutes late or they'd actually throw you out of the place. You couldn't talk....You couldn't even go to the bathroom. We were treated like slaves. I worked for Scher Brothers—a place people of my generation never forgot. He was a real slavedriver. He used to pick people from the boat and use them for slavery. But people had to earn. So when you want to earn your own, you take anything.

Still, many of the women took pride in their work. Adriana Valenti told an interviewer:

I'd make up stories in my mind while I'm working. I'd say, "What kind of a person's going to wear this dress? Is she in good health, is she a good person? Where is she going to go?... Will she just throw this dress aside?" [laughs]...because on each ticket you put your name or number so you know who made it. Like you're creating something and someone is going to enjoy it. And then I'd think—what kind of a person? Is she going to be careful? Is she going to keep it well? It's not mine. I only made it and got paid for it.

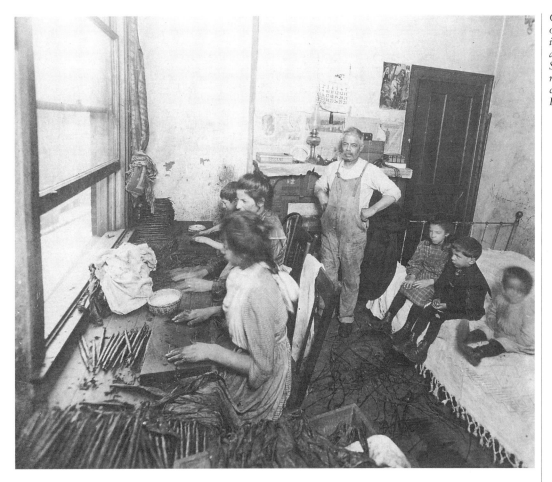

Cigar making was one of the trades that Italian immigrants adopted in the United States. This family rolled Toscani brand cigars in their home in Pittsburgh.

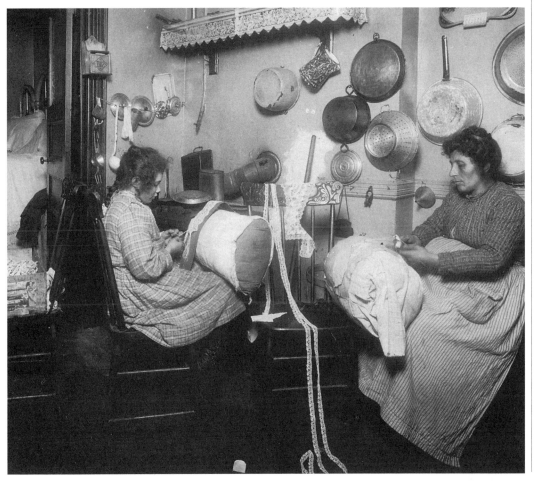

Italian women had made fine lace since the 16th century. Immigrants like this woman and her daughter, in a New York tenement in 1911, found a market for the skills that had been handed down in their families for generations.

57

FIGHTING FOR THE UNION

This magazine showed Massachusetts National Guardsmen pointing their bayonets at a group of strikers outside a Lawrence mill. Reports of brutal actions against strikers and their families caused Congress to investigate mill conditions.

In 1912, Lawrence, Massachusetts, produced more cloth than any other city in the world. Its textile mills employed more than 50,000 men, women, and children. Most of the workers were immigrants, among them many Italians. When the state government reduced the workweek from 56 hours to 54, the textile companies cut the workers' wages. The workers went on strike, and violence followed. Police beat the picketing strikers, and families began to send their children out of the city to protect them from harm. The Lawrence city government ordered that no more children could be evacuated. Two companies of the state militia and 50 policemen attacked a crowd of women and children at the train station. These events brought the Lawrence strike to the attention of Congress, which opened hearings on the condition of the mills and the treatment of the workers.

A 14-year-old girl named Camella Teoli was one of those who testified at the congressional hearings.

CHAIRMAN: *Now, did you ever get hurt in the mill?*
TEOLI: Yes.

C: *Tell us about it now, in your own way.*
TEOLI: Well, I used to go to school, and then a man came up to my house and asked my father why I didn't go to work, so

Many of the workers in the clothing mills were children like Camella Teoli. During the Lawrence, Massachusetts, strike in 1912, this parade of child laborers marched through the streets to win sympathy for their plight.

my father says I don't know whether she is 13 or 14 years old. [Workers, by state law, had to be 14.] So, the man say you give me $4 and I will make the papers come from the old country saying you are 14. So my father gave him the $4 and in one month came the papers that I was 14. I went to work and [in] about two weeks got hurt in my head....

C: *What part of your head?*
TEOLI: My head.

C: *Well, how were you hurt?*
TEOLI: The machine pulled my scalp off.

C: *The machine pulled your scalp off?*
TEOLI: Yes sir.

C: *How long ago was that?*
TEOLI: A year ago, or about a year ago.

C: *Were you in the hospital after that?*
TEOLI: I was in the hospital seven months.

Camella Teoli went back to the mills after the strike was over, and continued to do piecework until she was 60. She died in 1962.

Then, in 1980, Camella's children, Josephine Catalano and Frankie Palumbo, stood on the city commons of Lawrence, Massachusetts, to hear their mother's words read to a celebrating crowd. This was Bread and Roses Day, the commemoration of one of the most famous strikes in American history. Most of its leaders and many of the striking workers were Italian Americans, men, women, and children.

Arturo Giovanitti and Joseph Ettor

When the strike began in Lawrence, Massachusetts, several leaders of the Industrial Workers of the World (IWW) arrived to help organize the workers. Among them were two Italian-Americans, Arturo Giovannitti and Joseph Ettor.

The mill owners hoped to starve the strikers into submission, so Giovannitti organized soup kitchens to distribute food. Ettor, known as Smilin' Joe, moved through the city's neighborhoods with an interpreter, to encourage the workers from many nations—Italians, Poles, Germans, French, Lithuanians, Portuguese, and Syrians—to keep faith in the strike.

On January 29, a young Italian striker named Anna Lo Pezzi was shot during a confrontation between police and strikers. Though Giovannitti and Ettor were not present, the city charged them as accessories to her murder. Their arrest set off demonstrations both in the United States and abroad. Pittsburgh's Italian American community contributed to the defense fund for the IWW organizers.

At the trial, Giovannitti told the court: "I learned at my mother's knee to revere the name of a republic.... I ask the District Attorney, who speaks about the New England tradition...if he means the traditions...where they used to burn the witches at the stake, or if he means the New England traditions of those men who refused to be any longer under the iron heel of the British authority and dumped the tea into Boston Harbor.... History shall give its last word to us." After a two-month trial, Giovannitti and Ettore were acquitted.

Shortly before their release, the strikers celebrated their own victory. The mill owners ended the strike by granting pay raises, overtime pay, and improvements in working conditions.

Italian and Jewish garment workers demonstrate in New York's Union Square in 1913 with signs in Italian and Hebrew. Two of the garment workers' early union leaders were Luigi Antonini of the International Ladies Garment Workers Union and Frank Bellanca of the Amalgamated Clothing Workers of America.

During the 1890s, at least 22 Italians in the United States were lynched. The most famous case took place in New Orleans. In October 1890, a gang of five men shot David Hennessy, the city's superintendent of police. As he was dying, Hennessy supposedly accused Italians of the crime, but did not name any. The police rounded up more than 100 Italians as suspects, and nine were finally put on trial.

The trial was conducted in an atmosphere of hostility and prejudice against the Italians, who were mainly from Sicily. Sicilians had been coming to New Orleans since before the Civil War, finding success in the fishing industry and the business of importing fruits from Central America.

Even before Hennessy's murder, rumors had spread through the city about the Mafia, a secret organization of Italian criminals. Civic leaders blamed the Mafia for the city's crime and other problems. Now the newspapers fanned the prejudice against the accused Italians. Yet at their trial the evidence against them was so flimsy that the jury found them not guilty.

The verdict enraged the populace. Encouraged by the newspapers, they decided to take the law into their own hands. A vigilance committee was formed on March 13, 1891. On the next day, local citizens stormed the New Orleans jail. Among the mob were so-called respectable doctors and lawyers. They hanged two of the suspects and shot nine other Italian prisoners to death.

These barbarous acts brought an official protest from the Italian government. For a time there was even talk of war between the two countries. But no one in the mob was ever brought to justice. And the opinion of many Americans was that the victims got what they deserved. The venerable *New York Times* editorialized, "Those sneaking and cowardly Sicilians...are to us a pest without mitigation.... The Lynch Law was the only course open to the people of New Orleans."

THE BURDEN OF PREJUDICE

John Fante wrote several novels about Italian American life, drawing on his own experiences. He described the feelings caused by taunts from the local Irish grocer.

I don't like the grocer. My mother sends me to his store every day, and instantly he chokes up my breathing with the greeting, "Hellow, you little Dago! What'll you have?" So I detest him, and never enter his store if other customers are to be seen, for to be called a Dago before others is a ghastly, almost a physical humiliation. My stomach expands and recedes, and I feel naked....

During a ball game on the school grounds, a boy who plays on the opposing team begins to ridicule my playing. It is the ninth inning, and I ignore his taunts. We are losing the game, but if I can knock out a hit our chances of winning are pretty strong. I am determined to come through, and I face the pitcher confidently. The tormentor sees me at the plate.

"Ho! Ho!" he shouts. "Look who's up! The Wop's up. Let's get rid of the Wop."

This is the first time anyone at school has ever flung the word at me, and I am so angry that I strike out foolishly. We fight after the game, this boy and I, and I make him take it back.

Now school days become fighting days. Nearly every afternoon at 3:15 a crowd gathers to watch me make some guy take it back. This is fun; I am getting somewhere now, so come on, you guys, I dare you to call me a Wop!

For an elderly Italian woman who was interviewed in the 1970s, the bitter memories of the prejudice she experienced as a new immigrant remained strong.

During the winter, it was the worst time. You could hardly go out. My mother used to wear those heavy, warm shawls. They turned out to be protection for more than just the cold. My mother would huddle into the shawl when she went out, and then the snowballs would start flying. Sometimes they hit her so hard, she was afraid to walk. And those who threw them shouted, "guinea, guinea," and followed her down the street.... My mother would pretend she had a knife in her pocket sometime, just to scare them off. They *were* scared, too, especially because they expected Italians to carry knives in those days.

Fiorello La Guardia's father, an immigrant, became a bandmaster in the U.S. Army, and Fiorello grew up at an army post in Arizona. There, as he recalled in his autobiography:

I must have been about ten when a street organ-grinder with a monkey blew into town. He, and particularly the monkey, attracted a great deal of attention. I can still hear the cries of the kids: "A dago with a monkey! Hey, Fiorello, you're a dago, too. Where's your monkey?" It hurt.... I couldn't understand it. What difference was there between us? Some of their families hadn't been in the country any longer than mine.

On April 15, 1920, the paymaster and a guard at a shoe factory in South Braintree, Massachusetts, were murdered in a robbery. Soon, two naturalized Italian immigrants, Nicola Sacco and Bartolomeo Vanzetti, were arrested and charged with the crime. Sacco and Vanzetti were anarchists, followers of a radical political philosophy that opposed all forms of government. Along with their Italian heritage, this made them vulnerable to the antiforeign and antiradical hysteria that followed World War I.

After a trial conducted by a judge who was openly hostile to Italians, Sacco and Vanzetti were found guilty and sentenced to death. For six years, their sentence was appealed to higher courts. Despite widespread protests both in the United States and Europe, Sacco and Vanzetti were executed on August 27, 1927, still maintaining their innocence.

Though neither man had much education—Sacco worked in a shoe factory and Vanzetti was a fish peddler—they won widespread sympathy by their heartfelt statements during the trial and afterward.

At his sentencing, Bartolomeo Vanzetti declared:

Not only am I innocent of these two crimes, not only in all my life I have never stole, never killed, never spilled blood, but I have struggled all my life, since I began to reason, to eliminate crime from the earth.

Everybody that knows these two arms knows very well that I did not need to go in between the street and kill a man to take the money....

We have proved that there could not have been another judge on the face of the earth more prejudiced and more cruel than you have been against us. We have proven that. Still they refuse the new trial. We know, and you know in your heart, that you have been against us from the very beginning, before you see us. Before you see us you already know that we were radicals....

I am suffering because I am a radical and indeed I am a radical; I have suffered because I was an Italian, and indeed I am an Italian; I have suffered more for my family and for my beloved than for myself; but I am so convinced to be right that if you could execute me two times, and if I could be reborn two other times, I would live again to do what I have done already.

I have finished. Thank you.

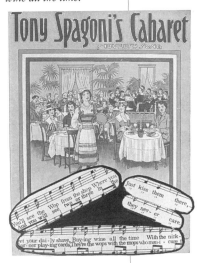

Some popular songs used ethnic stereotypes, as in this one depicting an Italian restaurant where "You'll see the Wop from the shop...buying wine all the time."

During the trial of Sacco and Vanzetti, the judge told a friend he "would get them good and proper"; he later gave them the death sentence. On August 23, 1977, the 50th anniversary of their execution, Governor Michael Dukakis of Massachusetts issued a posthumous pardon for the two men.

Andrea Sbarbaro

Andrea Sbarbaro was a dreamer and an idealist. What he originally planned as an ideal community turned into the Italian Swiss Colony wine empire. Sbarbaro was one of the pioneers in what is today one of California's most important industries.

Sbarbaro was born in Genoa and went to San Francisco as a young man in 1852. Right away his idealism showed itself. He founded savings and loans associations where Italian immigrants could place their savings and borrow money to buy land and equipment to farm. Believing fervently in the value of education, he opened a night school for immigrants so they could learn English. He even wrote special textbooks for them to use.

His success as a banker enabled him to enter a new venture in 1881. Sbarbaro bought land in Sonoma County and called the area Asti after a grape-growing region of northern Italy. Sbarbaro's dream was that all the workers would own some of the shares of the venture. "I told them," he later wrote, "that their wages would be from thirty to forty dollars a month, with good food, wine at their meals,…and comfortable houses to sleep in. But in order to inspire an interest in the work and desiring that the Colony should be strictly cooperative, I explained that each laborer must subscribe to at least five shares of stock."

The workers balked at the idea of deducting money from their pay to buy the shares. Sbarbaro was disappointed, but he relented and the workers labored for wages alone.

The early years were hard. After the vines were planted, phylloxera [plant insects] attacked them. Flooding from the Russian River threatened the crop. Still the colony persevered and finally the grapes were harvested. By this time, however, the market price of grapes had dropped drastically, so Sbarbaro decided to make wine with them.

The colony at Asti now began to prosper. Neat homes and schools were provided for the workers. Soon a church and an electric plant were built. Sbarbaro introduced new plants and trees that had never grown in the region before—such as oranges, limes, pomegranates, chestnuts, and olives.

Sbarbaro's triumph was complete in 1911 when the Italian Swiss Colony champagne won the Grand Prix at the International Fair in Turin, Italy. It was the first time that an American champagne had won such an award.

SUCCESS STORIES IN THE WEST

Italians had settled in the western part of the United States by the mid-19th century. They were among the early pioneers, land holders, merchants, and adventurers. There were Italian settlers in Texas while it was still part of Mexico. Prospero Bernardi fought at the Battle of San Jacinto, in which Texas won its independence from Mexico.

By and large, Italian Americans in California, who were originally attracted by the gold rush and wine industry, were more prosperous than those who lived in the Little Italys of East Coast cities. In 1905, Marius J. Spinello, a professor at the University of California, wrote glowingly about the California Italians.

California has nearly sixty thousand Italian citizens and…the economic conditions of the Italian population in this state are incomparably better than those of the Italians in the east....

San Francisco has many a brilliant and highly respected professional man of Italian birth or parentage. The beautiful orchards, vineyards and gardens planted by Italians on the shifting sand dunes of San Francisco, of San Mateo, in Santa Clara valley, around Stockton, Napa, Fresno, Tulare, Los Angeles, and on the slopes of the Sierras, tell us what the sturdy sons of the noble nation to which the world is indebted for all that makes life worth living, can do wherever their lot is cast, and especially under the mild and benignant sky of California. Everywhere, we are told, the most well-kept vineyards, most luxuriant and profitable orchards belong to Italians....

The eastern Italian comes from the same country and stock from which the California Italian comes, but though very successful, he has not been able to accomplish so much in so short

Members of the Italian Swiss Colony at Asti, California, enjoy a dinner around 1910. Note the light bulb hanging over the table, the result of Andrea Sbarbaro's installation of an electric generator.

a time. Why? Because, in the east, he found the country thickly populated and had to begin his climbing at the lowest step of the ladder, while the people who had come before him, were well-nigh the top. In California, on the other hand, he came as early as the rest of the early settlers and stared alongside of them. Here, he met with no race prejudice. The virgin soil was as responsive to his toiling as it was to the labors of others. And today he finds himself on equal footing with all the other inhabitants of California.

A. P. Giannini foresaw that the fledgling movie industry would be immensely profitable. His bank lent money to the moviemaker Cecil B. deMille in 1923, enabling him to finish The Ten Commandments, one of the first big-budget movies. Here, Giannini gives a "leg up" to help child movie star Jackie Coogan deposit his salary check.

Salvatore Lucchese, shown here with his sons Sam (right) and Frank, was born into a family of boot makers in Sicily. After coming to the United States as a teenager, Lucchese opened a boot shop in San Antonio, Texas, in 1883 that became widely known for the quality of its boots. Theodore Roosevelt outfitted his Rough Riders there during the Spanish-American War of 1898. Lucchese's children took over the firm after his death in 1929. During World War II Generals Dwight Eisenhower and George S. Patton wore Lucchese boots, as did cowboy movie star Gene Autry. President Lyndon Johnson took his pair to the White House. Today, the Lucchese name continues to stand for quality footwear.

A. P. Giannini

When the Great Earthquake shook San Francisco on April 18, 1906, A. P. Giannini was 17 miles away. The six-foot, two-inch Italian American started on foot toward San Francisco. By noon, he reached the modest offices of his Bank of Italy in North Beach, the Italian area of the city. With a few trusted employees, Giannini placed the deposits—about $80,000 in gold—into orange crates, which he loaded onto a shabby horse-drawn wagon. Giannini's decisive actions that day helped him to build one of the biggest banks in the world.

The son of immigrants from Liguria in northern Italy, Amadeo Peter Giannini received his first name as a reminder of the old country, and his second as an "American" name. At age seven, Amadeo saw his father stabbed to death in a dispute with a neighbor.

His mother remarried and the family moved to San Francisco. Amadeo went to work for his stepfather, who owned a wholesale produce business in North Beach. Dealing with the Italian farmers of the region, Amadeo saw that regular banks were reluctant to loan them money. So in 1904, he opened his Banca d'Italia inside an old saloon. The bank was staffed completely by Italians, and Giannini personally greeted each customer.

The day after the earthquake, Giannini's bank was the first in the city to reopen. From an outdoor desk made of two barrels and a plank, Giannini stood ready to pay his depositors with the gold he had rescued. He offered loans to people who were in desperate need and had nothing to offer as security. His customers never forgot it.

Giannini had another new idea—branch banks to make it easier for customers in different areas to do their banking. He opened his first one at San Jose, in the Santa Clara valley, where he had grown up. Whenever a customer came in with a child, Giannini would present the parents with a dollar and suggest that they open a savings account for their little one. By 1919, the Bank of Italy had the largest number of depositors of any American bank.

In 1928, Giannini bought a New York bank called the Bank of America, a name he then took for his own network of banks. The Bank of America expanded to become the largest privately owned bank in the world. Before his death in 1949, Giannini was asked the secret of his success. "Well," he answered, "we were new to the game when we started out; we did unusual things."

Antonio and Sebastiana Fricano, with their daughter Rose. The family came from Sicily to the United States in 1907. This photo was taken three years later.

CHAPTER FIVE

LA VIA NUOVA

For Italian immigrants, *la via nuova*, "the new way," was primarily an urban experience. When Giuseppe Garibaldi arrived in New York City's Staten Island in 1852, there was already a sizable colony of Italians living in the city. In that same decade, Italian fishermen settled in the North Beach area of San Francisco, where generations of their descendants continue to live.

When the great wave of immigration began, many Italians found lodgings close to where the ferry dropped them off—in the Mulberry district of Manhattan. In time, Mulberry Street would become the heart of what is called Little Italy. Here, newcomers often found relatives and fellow-villagers to help them get a start in America. In the streets they heard the sounds of their familiar language, found shops that sold foods they knew from home, and experienced the security of living among their *paesani*.

Before Italians arrived, the Mulberry district had been a slum where few people dared to walk at night. The peasants from the Mezzogiorno turned it into a neighborhood—still poor, but one where the streets teemed with life and activity. Organ grinders played the sentimental songs of the old country, and pushcart vendors advertised their wares with shouts that reached to the upper-story windows of the tenements.

To escape their crowded, airless apartments, the immigrants spent as much time outside as possible. In the evenings, women sat on the fire escapes, the roofs, and the stone stoops, chatting with their friends. Men found a vacant lot for a *bocce* court (a game played with small bowling balls) or played card games such as *scopa*. For the children, the streets were their playground, and they improvised games such as stickball, a street form of baseball that used sewer covers and curbstones as boundaries. It was no coincidence that one of the first American sports in which Italians excelled was baseball.

In the years from 1880 to 1930, the nation's largest city was also its fastest-growing urban area. Italians helped to construct modern-day New York's skyscrapers, bridges, tunnels, subways, and streets.

So many Italians arrived that Little Italy was unable to hold them all. When the Brooklyn Bridge was built in 1883—in part by Italian laborers—Italians used it to move into other neighborhoods across the East River. Italians also moved uptown—in the subways that they helped to build—to neighborhoods in East Harlem and the Bronx, and—using tunnels or bridges that they had also worked on—across the Hudson River into communities in New Jersey.

New York City contained the largest number of Italian immigrants, but Little Italys sprang up in other cities as well. By 1900 the Philadelphia neighborhood known as South Philly was the second-largest Italian American community. Other sizable Italian neighborhoods were found in Boston's North End, the Near West Side of Chicago (Little Sicily), the port area of Baltimore, St. Louis ("Dago Hill"), and San Francisco's North Beach.

Within these tightly knit communities, the customs and traditions of the old country could be preserved and guarded from what many Italians saw as the corrupting influence of American society. As Rudolph J. Vecoli, a historian and son of Italian immigrants, wrote: "What [the immigrants] learned of this strange country often repelled them. From their perspective the *'Mericani* appeared a foolish people, without a sense of humor, respect, or proper behavior....Efforts on the part of teachers and social workers to Americanize them and their children were resented as intrusions on the sovereignty of the family."

For—in the United States, as it had been in Italy—*la famiglia* was the strongest social unit. The father was unquestionably the head of the family, but the mother was its center. Father's duty was to provide for his wife and children, to protect and to guard them, and to make decisions that affected their welfare. But within the home Mother reigned. She managed the financial affairs, governed the conduct of her children, and provided the warmth and security that gave the family its strength. The long hours she spent preparing the sumptuous meals that are an Italian tradition were a sign of her devotion—as well as a source of pride. She deferred to her husband because conflict within the family was regarded as her disgrace. She demanded obedience from her children because when they strayed from *la via vecchia* (the old way), it reflected badly on the mother.

Yet inevitably the second generation of Italian Americans did become Americanized. In school, they were looked down on because they were Italian. Instead of rejecting the teachers' opinions, they resented their parents. As Leonard Covello, an immigrant son who became a great educator, wrote, "We were becoming American by learning to be ashamed of our parents."

For boys, traditionally permitted more freedom in the Italian family, the transition to American life was easier than for their sisters. Daughters resented their parents' insistence that every time they associated with a young man, a chaperone had to be present. When a family saved enough to send a child to college, the sons had first priority—for the daughters' destiny was to marry and raise families. Sometimes from necessity, but often by choice, the daughters took jobs, despite their parents' disapproval. Even then, they were

An Italian grocer at First Avenue and 10th Street in New York City in 1943.

expected to turn their wages over to their mothers to supplement the family income.

The church was a source of strength for many Italian immigrants, most of whom were Roman Catholic. But their version of Catholicism was very different from that practiced by earlier Roman Catholic immigrants, notably the Irish. Over the centuries, the peasants of the Mezzogiorno had developed their own religious practices, usually devotions to the Virgin Mary or to the patron saint of their village church. Processions on the saint's feast day wound through the streets of the village. Families built shrines to the saints in their fields and homes, fervently believing that prayer would bring help.

Many Italians brought these practices to the new country, only to find that the priests here disapproved of them. The Roman Catholic Church in the United States was dominated by Irish American priests and bishops. No Italian American became a cardinal of the Church until 1982, when Archbishop Joseph Bernardin of Chicago, the son of an immigrant stonecutter, received that honor. The Irish clergy had a stricter view of what "proper" worship should be. They were appalled to see Italians approach the statues of saints and physically kiss and caress them, asking for favors.

Furthermore, there was a strong Italian tradition of anti-clericalism (hostility to the clergy), which immigrants brought with them. Dating from the time when the pope was Italy's largest landholder, anticlericalism increased when the pope stood in the way of Italian unification. Already distrustful of priests, who had often been their landlords in Italy, the peasants of the Messogiorno felt no kinship with the Irish-American clergy. Conflict with the Irish-dominated American church caused many Italian immigrants to shun the American Catholic school system, sending their children to the public schools.

Immigrants built their own

churches, often named after the same saint they had revered in Italy. The annual processions, accompanied by a *festa* of food and joyous celebration, became a hallmark of Little Italys.

An Italian bishop, Giovanni Baptiste Scalabrini, founded a society to minister to the Italians who had emigrated. One of Bishop Scalabrini's followers, Francesca Cabrini, arrived in New York in 1889. She established many hospitals, schools, and social-service agencies for newly arrived immigrants—and for her work was canonized as the first American saint in 1946.

Likewise, Italian Americans began their own secular institutions. Many were mutual aid societies that provided life insurance and hospital care for their members, who paid dues of thirty to sixty cents a month. The clubhouses of these societies became community meeting places and sponsored athletic teams and social events. The membership often consisted of those who shared a common background in an Italian village or province.

In 1905, Dr. Vincenzo Sellaro founded the Order of the Sons of Italy, which grew into a national organization with more than 1,300 branches throughout the nation. The Sons of Italy often attracted the most successful Italian American business leaders, lawyers, and doctors.

The first Italian-language newspaper in the United States, the weekly *L'Eco d'Italia*, started publication in 1849. Thirty years later, a daily Italian American newspaper, *Il Progresso Italo-Americano*, made its appearance in New York City. Still published today, *Il Progresso* grew into the largest and most influential Italian American publication under the ownership of Generoso Pope, one of the first Italian American millionaires.

More than 2,000 Italian Ameri-

The DiCostanzos, owners of a Mulberry Street restaurant in New York's Little Italy, greet the arrival of the new year on December 31, 1942.

can newspapers have been published at various times in cities all over the country. Printing news of events in Italy, they were among the links between Italian Americans and the home country. Many Italian immigrants retained a sense of dual identity, preserving their Italian traditions within *la via nuova*. Those who had attained prosperity in their new country sent money to relatives back home and contributed generously to Italian disaster victims.

When Benito Mussolini came to power in Italy in 1922, many Italian Americans rejoiced, for Mussolini promised prosperity and strong leadership. Mussolini's Fascist Party used symbols that reminded Italians, and Italian Americans, of their ancient heritage as citizens of the Roman Empire. He also pleased Italian Americans by settling Italy's dispute with the Catholic Church, which had continued since the Risorgimento. In 1929, Mussolini signed the Lateran Treaty, in which Pope Pius XI finally gave up the Church's claim to Italian territory in return for a payment from Mussolini's government. In addition, the treaty gave the area around the pope's residence in Rome the status of an independent state, Vatican City.

However, Mussolini became a dictator, ruthlessly stamping out opposition to his regime. Many Italian political exiles fled to the United States, where they spoke out against the evils of fascism. After Mussolini allied his country with Adolf Hitler and Nazi Germany, Italy passed a series of anti-Semitic laws. When Mussolini joined in the Nazi invasion of France, his support among Italian Americans declined.

After the United States entered World War II in 1941, its citizens of Italian heritage swiftly showed their loyalty by volunteering for the armed forces. Few hesitated in making the choice between the new country and the old. The Italian immigrants and their children had become part of America.

LITTLE ITALY

On hot summer days in the immigrant neighborhoods, people escaped from their tiny, stifling apartments by sitting on the sidewalk and chatting with neighbors. In New York's Little Italy around 1910, an old man watches over his grandchild.

Mario Manzardo's parents came from Italy in the early part of the 20th century. They settled south of Chicago, in the community of Pullman, a "company town" named for the railroad-car manufacturer for which most of the people of the town worked. Mario recalled:

My father] settled down in the forge shop of the Pullman Car Works, a worker with three growing children, a mortgage on a Pullman house, a golden voice and a great love for opera.

Most of our *paesani* and friends were music lovers. They had formed amateur singing and dramatic groups, and performed in the local halls for over a quarter of a century. Often the proceeds of the singing and dramatic "festa" would go to labor causes: the Ettor and Giovannitti defense; Sacco and Vanzetti; Tom Mooney, others.

Father sang baritone, a sweet, lusty voice. He could sing the entire role of Rigoletto and performed duets with his friend, Gildo Padovan, a tenor. They sang from the music of

In densely populated urban neighborhoods, children used the street as a playground. Sometimes barriers were set up to block traffic and create "play streets." Here, in the 1930s on 108th Street in Manhattan, a boy prepares to dodge a ball thrown by his opponent.

Puccini, Donizetti, Verdi.... Together they sang beautiful stirring Verdi choruses as well as melodic mountain tunes of the Veneto [in northern Italy]. How well I remember the glorious workers' songs they sang: the "Inno dei Lavatori" ["Workers' Hymn"] and other union and socialist anthems, the old patriotic "Inno di Garibaldi," "Fratelli d'Italia." These, my father sang together with his *paesani* and friends.

But more often they would get together in a home—many times ours—on cold winter Saturday nights. There were songs, new and old; chestnuts roasting in the oven; the Zinfandel wine flowing; black bitter coffee laced with grappa [grape brandy] and often a surprise: *Spaghetti al olio e sardella* at midnight....

In the spring of 1936, on the first day of May, my father joined the Italian chorus on the stage of the Venetian Hall in Kensington. On this gala occasion they sang:

Viei, o Maggio; t'aspettan le genti,
Ti salutano i liberi cuori,
Dolce pasqua del lavatori....

[Come, oh May Day; the people await you,
The liberated hearts salute you,
Sweet Easter of the working class....]

This was the last time my father sang in public.
It happened at work in the shop just before the noon

In 1888, photographer Lewis Hine set up his camera at the entrance to 39 1/2 Mulberry Street, an alley in New York's Little Italy. Though Hine was generally sympathetic to the immigrants, he titled this photo "Bandit's Roost."

The journalist Jacob Riis described the Feast of San Donato in New York in 1899:

All the sheets of the tenement had been stretched so as to cover the ugly sheds and outhouses. Against the dark rear tenement the shrine of the saint had been erected, shutting it altogether out of sight with a wealth of scarlet and gold. Great candles and little ones, painted and beribboned, burned in a luminous grove before the altar. The sun shone down upon a mass of holiday-clad men and women, to whom it was all as a memory of home, of the beloved home across the seas....The fire-escapes of the tenement had, with the aid of some cheap muslin draperies, a little tinsel, and the strange artistic genius of this people, been transformed into beautiful balconies, upon which the tenants of the front house had reserved seats. In a corner of the yard over by the hydrant, a sheep, which was to be raffled off as the climax of the celebration, munched its wisp of hay patiently, while bare-legged children climbed its back and pulled its wool. From the second story of the adjoining house, which was a stable, a big white horse stuck his head at intervals out of the window, and surveyed the shrine and the people with an interested look.

The musicians...blew "Santa Lucia" on their horns. The sweetly seductive melody woke the echoes of the block and its slumbering memories. The old women rocked in their seats, their faces buried in their hands. The crowd from the street increased, and the chief celebrant, who turned out to be no less a person than the saloon-keeper himself, reaped a liberal harvest of silver half-dollars. The villagers bowed and crossed themselves before the saint, and put into the plate their share toward the expenses of the celebration.

Milwaukee's St. Rocco Mutual Aid Society prepares to celebrate the feast of its patron saint in August 1928. Groups like these offered many benefits—insurance, financial aid in times of need, and perhaps most important, friends and business contacts who shared a similar background.

whistle. They carried him home on a litter. "Cerebrovascular hemorrhage," the doctor said. "Keep him quiet. Don't waste your money on a hospital. Nothing can be done." We propped him up in bed to make him comfortable. His mute mouth attempted a twisted smile.

We rolled the old Victrola to the door of the bedroom. After winding the old spring motor I carefully placed the needle into the groove. The record was a favorite operatic aria. Tears welled up into his eyes. We turned off the disc fearing we had caused trauma. He moved his good arm up and down, beating against the mattress. His intelligent eyes became opaque as with anger. I placed the needle back in the groove and the music started again. His eyes cleared. His lips attempted to form the words he had sung numberless times. But no sound came out of his mouth.

Mario Puzo, the son of Neapolitan immigrants, described growing up in Hell's Kitchen, the Italian and Irish neighborhood on the West Side of Manhattan.

My family and I grew up together on Tenth Avenue, between Thirtieth and Thirty-First Streets, part of the area called Hell's Kitchen. This particular neighborhood could have been a movie set for one of the Dead End Kids flicks or for the social drama of the East Side in which John Garfield played the hero. Our tenements were the western wall of the city. Beneath our windows were the vast black iron gardens of the New York Central Railroad, absolutely blooming with stinking boxcars freshly unloaded of cattle and pigs for the city slaughterhouse. Steers sometimes escaped and loped through the heart of the neighborhood, followed by astonished young boys who had never seen a live cow....

I never came home to an empty house; there was always the smell of supper cooking. My mother was always there to greet me, sometimes with a policeman's club in her hand (nobody ever knew how she acquired it). But she was always there, or her authorized deputy, my older sister, who preferred throwing empty milk bottles at the heads of her little brothers when they got bad marks on their report cards. During the Great Depression of the 1930s, though we were the poorest of the poor, I never remember not dining well. Many years later as a guest of a millionaire's club, I realized that our poor family on home relief ate better than some of the richest people in America.

My mother would never dream of using anything but the best imported olive oil, the best Italian cheeses. My father had access to the fruits coming off ships, the produce from railroad cars, all before it went through the stale process of middlemen; and my mother, like most Italian women, was a fine cook in the peasant style.

Puzo recalled the happy days he spent at the Hudson Guild Settlement House in his neighborhood.

Mulberry Street, the heart of New York's Little Italy, as it looked in 1906. Near the awnings at right is a sign marking the Banca Nalzone, an Italian-owned bank where immigrants could send money orders to their families in Italy.

Most people do not know that a settlement house is really a club combined with social service. The Hudson Guild, a five-story field of joy for slum kids, had ping pong rooms and billiard rooms, a shop in which to make lamps, a theater for putting on amateur plays, a gym to box and play basketball in....

There were young men who guided us as counselors whom I remember with fondness to this day. They were more like friends than adults assigned to watch over us. I still remember one helping us eat a box of stolen chocolates rather than reproaching us. Which was exactly the right thing for him to do; we trusted him after that. The Hudson Guild kept more kids out of jail than a thousand policemen. It still exists today, functioning for the new immigrants, the blacks, and the Puerto Ricans.

Shopping in Little Italy often involved an elaborate system of bargaining over the price, as Richard Gambino recalled.

My grandmother would walk into a store or shop, ignore the proprietor—in our area virtually always Italian—and peruse the shop's merchandise with the most casual, haphazard manner she could affect. In the custom of the old land it was her role not to seem terribly interested in buying and certainly not to tip what she was after. And it was the merchant's role to guess exactly what she wanted. After a while, my grandmother would begin to ask the prices of items

There were many ways for immigrant children to contribute to their families' incomes. The boy at center obtained loaves of stale bread from a bakery, which he sold in the street.

A street vendor opens fresh clams for his customers in Little Italy in New York. Shellfish brought back memories of home for many Italian Americans, particularly those who came from the island of Sicily or from the coastal areas of Italy.

she fingered suspiciously, indicating that they were obviously inferior. In response to his replies, she would immediately unhand the item in question, her every facial and bodily nuance saying it was repulsive in quality and its price a moral outrage. After these unhurried preliminaries, bargaining would begin in earnest over the real object of her interest...starting at outlandish extremes, she and the merchant would bark out final prices.

An Italian American woman recalled the first lodgings she and her husband had in the new country.

We had a sink in the hall with nothing else, and four families to share it. And one bathroom in the yard where garbage was also thrown. How could a body wash and have a bit of privacy that way? I died a little everytime I went there.

Mono Cino, a retired construction worker, described the first place his family lived in Little Italy after their arrival in 1910.

I don't know how we found it but we lived in a small short alley, it's still there, called Extra Place, near the Bowery on First Street. I remember the cobblestones, and you could smell what everybody was cooking. The halls were lit by gas jets. The toilets were made of cast iron and were in the halls.

For many immigrants, the struggle to survive was difficult. The strain can be seen on the face of the woman at center, in a Chicago tenement house in 1910.

Constantine Panunzio, who first saw the North End of Boston in 1902, reported that conditions had changed greatly when he revisited it 12 years later.

For one thing, here was a congestion the like of which I had never seen before. Within the narrow limits of one-half square mile were crowded together 35,000 people, living tier upon tier, huddled together until the very heavens seemed to be shut out. These narrow alley-like streets of Old Boston were one mass of litter. The air was laden with soot and dirt. Ill odors arose from every direction. Here was no trees; no parks worthy of the name; no playgrounds other than the dirty streets for the children to play on; no birds to sing their songs; no flowers to waft their perfume; and only small strips of sky to be seen; while around the entire neighborhood like a mighty cordon, a thousand wheels of commercial activity whirled incessantly day and night, making noises which would rack the sturdiest of nerves.

Some Italians were intimidated by the Mano Nera, *or "Black Hand." It was a criminal gang whose members preyed on immigrants. They left their mark—the imprint of a sooty black hand—on notes making demands for money. The Black Hand notes were often left by lawless individuals who took advantage of the widespread fear associated with the gang. Over time, copycats from other ethnic groups and even corrupt police officers used the same method and name. The following is a letter to the* New York Times *from a victim.*

My name is Salvatore Spinelli. My parents in Italy came from a decent family. I came here [to New York] eight years ago and went to work as a house painter, like my father. I started a family and I have been a citizen for thirteen years. My children all went to school as soon as they were old enough. I went into business. I began to think I was doing well. Everybody in my family was happy. I had a house at 314 East 11th Street and another one at 316, which I rented out. At this point the "Black Hand" came into my life and asked me for seven thousand dollars. I told them to go to hell and the bandits tried to blow up my house. Then I asked the police for help and refused more demands, but the Black Hand set one, two, three, four, five bombs in my houses. Things went to pieces. From 32 tenants I am down to six. I owe a thousand dollars interest that is due next month and I cannot pay. I am a ruined man. My family lives in fear. There is a policeman on guard in front of my house, but what can he do? My brother Francesco and I do guard duty at the windows with guns night and day. My wife and children have not left the house for weeks. How long is all this going on?

In 1894, an Italian American knife sharpener practiced his trade on the street. Many immigrants started their own businesses in ways such as this.

Ragpickers like these two men collected rags and old clothes, which were resold to paper manufacturers. Nothing of value was ever wasted in the immigrant communities.

One woman remembered her childhood in Little Italy, before automobiles had replaced horse-drawn carriages.

In the summer the streets were filled with horses. The horse manure was piled up in the gutter and it dried into powder and the wind blew it in the air and it covered your clothes, your hair, your face, and you couldn't hardly breathe. Opposite our place there was a barn with small elephants in it. Nobody knew what they were doing there. Late at night I could hear them crying. It was so sad.

Despite the hard work, amusements such as theater and dance halls were part of Italian American life. An old immigrant recalled preparing for Saturday night in the theater district around Second Avenue and 14th Street in New York.

We came home from work Saturday afternoon and the rest of the day we got ready. My brother Angelo worked in a laundry, but his heart was in dancing. Tony, my other brother, was the tallest, 6'1", well built, a little flat footed. He had the ambition to be a movie actor. He was a plasterer with *compare* [his friend] Toto. But Saturday afternoon we got ready; the suits were inspected, the shirts with detachable collars and cuffs were laid out, shoes well heeled and soled. Then we dressed in the dark bedroom where we all slept. We put on these elegant clothes: first the garters to hold up our black silk socks; suspenders, more comfortable for dancing;

over the shoes, spats; a tie pin and handkerchief in the breast pocket. I was the youngest and I'd go get the whiskey flask and the hand warmer, a small tin container covered with red felt with chunks of burning charcoal in it.

Alessandro Mastro-Valerio came to the United States in 1892 with plans to create a farming community for Italian immigrants in Alabama. The venture failed, and he settled in Chicago, where he eventually became editor of the newspaper La Tribuna Italia Transatlantico. *Just before the turn of the century, there were about 25,000 Italians living in the city. Mastro-Valerio disapproved of their "filthy" habits, which he attributed to the crowded conditions of city life and greed.*

The greed of gain...causes most of the women to employ all their spare time in sewing clothing, in order to add their little share to the earnings of the husband and sons. This is a serious detriment to them, and is one cause of their filthy homes, which they have no time to care for. By reason of the same greed, boys and girls are sent to sell newspapers in the streets, and sometimes to beg....

L'Italia, the leading Italian newspaper of Chicago, inaugurated with its first number a veritable crusade against the two offenses of ragpicking and sending boys and girls in the streets, and was instrumental in holding a mass-meeting for compulsory education in Chicago.... The mass-meeting ended in the appointment of a committee of prominent Italians to call upon Mayor Cregier and upon the [city] council, requesting the interference of the police in the ragpicking of the Italians. Briefly speaking, an ordinance was passed and enforced; but the ragpickers formed a sort of political association, and let the party in power understand that they were voters who would vote against the party at the next election if the interference of the police in their occupation was not stopped. Immediately the police, by secret orders, let the ragpickers alone. No lobbyists in Washington could have worked the scheme more effectually. This will answer the question whether Italians have Americanized themselves, and to what extent.

In Boston's North End around 1912, a girl and boy pose with their pet dog. Italian American neighbors watched out for each other's children in the streets of Little Italys. The cry, "I'll tell your mamma," was enough to stop any mischief.

Mother Cabrini

When Francesca Cabrini arrived in New York in March 1889, she stayed with five other nuns in a rented room infested by cockroaches and mice. A few months earlier, she had sat with Pope Leo XII in the Vatican Palace. The pope, concerned about Italians in the United States, asked Cabrini to go help them.

Born in Lombardy, Italy, on July 15, 1850, Francesca Cabrini grew up with the desire to serve others. She founded her own order of nuns in 1881, the Missionary Sisters of the Sacred Heart.

In New York's Little Italy, Cabrini saw that the people were desperately in need. The community lacked doctors, teachers, and even priests. Orphans roamed the streets. Cabrini had found her life's work. She opened a nursery in an empty store, started a sewing school, and taught a catechism class in a church basement. Tirelessly, she walked through the streets of Little Italy, asking merchants for donations and listening to the immigrants' problems.

Seeking a site for an orphanage, she raised money to buy an estate up the Hudson River. The price was low because the estate had to draw its water from the river. But on her second day there, she discovered a natural spring. God had provided.

In 1892, Mother Cabrini built a small hospital near Little Italy. She persuaded doctors to serve there part-time, without charging fees. All the nurses spoke Italian so the immigrants would feel comfortable. Because it was the 400th anniversary of Columbus's trip to America, she named the hospital after him. It would serve the "children of Columbus."

Mother Cabrini expanded her work into the many Little Italys in the United States. She traveled to New Orleans, where she comforted the families of the victims of the lynchings. When Mother Cabrini heard that the families of striking mine workers in Colorado needed food and clothing, she brought a shipment by train. She became an American citizen in 1909.

Mother Cabrini went to South America, where other Italians had immigrated. In Brazil, she contracted malaria but refused to rest. She died a few days before Christmas in 1917 while wrapping presents for children. She became a saint of the Roman Catholic church in 1946, the first U.S. citizen to be so honored.

LA FAMIGLIA

Josephine Fastuca was born to Italian immigrant parents in 1906 in Pittsburgh. Late in her life, she told an interviewer what her family life was like.

My father was a barber and my mother was a housewife. I went to Conroy school, which was a public school. I remember when we had parent-teacher meetings, my mother would never come, because she could not speak the language, and that was very disappointing for me. So when my children were growing up, I made sure that I was there. My children went to the same school that I did.

We had a big family in our house. We had a nephew of my father's, his brother's son, because the parents were dead. And my grandmother was living with us, and she had grandsons with her. And then we had my father's single brother, and that was the complete family.

We ate dinner together, and my mother naturally did the washing and ironing for all of them, and my grandmother would do most of the mending. She would set us on her knee and she would tell us stories, which we enjoyed very much, about the saints and different folklore from her village [in Italy].

A wedding party in Milwaukee in June 1924. Such festive occasions also provided an opportunity for unmarried young men and women to meet each other properly under the eyes of the elders.

One responsibility that I didn't like was ironing the barber-shop towels. That was my job. I tried to get out of it as many times as I could, but I didn't succeed. That was one job that I had to do. I never did any cooking, because in our house, you see, my dad did the cooking. He loved to do the cooking. He even made homemade noodles and all different kinds of food. In fact, I think he was a gourmet cook, really....Of course, my mother had a hard time cleaning afterwards, because men aren't very neat when they cook!

My mother never worked outside. She did sewing, though. She sewed if there were any women that wanted dresses made, or something like that. She would do that, besides sewing our clothes.

Sometimes my dad would play cards with his friends, and the men would put a small amount of money in the kitty. When they were through, they would go out and buy ice cream for the women and pitchers of beer for the men. And they would spend that money in the kitty.

On the holidays we would get together with the relatives. My father's sisters and brothers would come. Most of the time we had them at our home and we would eat our meals together. On Sundays we would go to church in the morning and then the family would gather together to have dinner and to play guitars and mandolins, and dance, mostly waltzes and polkas.

Jerre Mangione, a scholar and historian of the Italian American experience, described growing up in Rochester, New York, in the home of Sicilian immigrants.

As a young child constantly surrounded by Sicilian relatives, the public image of the Sicilians did not concern me much. A far greater worry was the question of who I was. It was a confusion I shared with my brothers and my sisters. Were we Americans or were we Sicilians? Neither our parents nor our teachers could provide us with an answer that satisfied any of us. Being the oldest child in the family, I was the first to be confused, especially as my first language was Sicilian. For reasons of love, our parents, who were afraid of losing communication with their own children, forbade us to speak English at home....

If we children had our own way, our parents would have dropped all of their Sicilian ideas and customs and behaved like "Americans." Like most children, we were mindless conformists. More than anything else, we wanted to be regarded as Americans, though we could not be certain what they were like. Among our relatives anyone who spoke English and was not an Italian was promptly categorized as an "American." Movie stars probably came closest to our conception of what Americans must be like. But in the face of having to speak Sicilian and eat Sicilian, it seemed futile to try to imitate them....

For my father and for many other Sicilian immigrant parents, the American world was fraught with alien mores that of-

Because the family was so important in the Italian tradition, those Italians who emigrated by themselves suffered great loneliness. Never was this greater than during the holidays. Joseph Talese, who emigrated in 1920, wrote in his diary:

This Christmas approaching, I was here all by myself. In my home, Christmastime, we had so many friends. And we go to church and we go singing carols. It was a great time. And here on Christmas Eve, I went to bed at 6:29, like a baby, I cry like a baby. I said, "I can't take it. I got to go back."

Rose Fricano with her doll in 1909, two years after she and her parents immigrated to the United States.

The wedding picture of Felix Ardemagni and Enrica Pianalto in Tontitown, Arkansas, around 1900. Whether the bride and groom were rich or poor, a wedding was cause for celebration.

fended them and corrupted their children. They were appalled, for example, that American boys and girls were permitted to date without having a chaperone along. In Sicily this would have been unthinkable. My relatives were also shocked to learn that American sons and daughters could become engaged and marry without obtaining permission from their parents. Such customs were antithetical to their own and, in their view, invariably destroyed the sanctity of the family and the authority of the father. In Sicily the father could expect (and receive) absolute obedience from every member of his family. Here he was relatively powerless; on reaching legal age, his children could do as they pleased....

Even though it meant living a double life—being Sicilian at home and American elsewhere—as children we enjoyed the company of our elders. It was only when they were being "Sicilian" in public that we felt embarrassed by them. I had a particular dread for picnics in public parks when Sicilian food was being consumed with pagan abandon, the sound of their talk and laughter drowning out all other sounds, while nearby some American family sat sedately and quietly nibbling on neatly trimmed sandwiches. Mistaking the high spirits and easy naturalness of my relatives for vulgarity, I worried about what the Americans might think of them, not realizing then that their reaction might be one of envy.

The poet John Ciardi remembered the two languages—one at home, the other at school.

In my childhood it was always two worlds. I have always felt that when you have a second language, you have three things: the first language, the second language, and the difference between them....I had to use a double standard: one thing out-of-doors and another thing indoors. It did not always work that way, that peaceably. Sometimes, in this generation gap, Italian boys especially, realizing that their parents were dead wrong, became nastily indignant. That led to shouting matches in which the kids and the father, sometimes the mother, said terrible things to one another. Two or three of the boys I grew up with ran away and were never heard from again.

Mario Puzo did not realize until after he was much older the meaning of his childhood impressions of his neighbors.

It did seem then that the Italian immigrants, all the fathers and mothers that I knew, were a grim lot; always shouting, always angry, quicker to quarrel than embrace. I did not understand that their lives were a long labor to earn their daily bread and that...fatigue does not sweeten human natures.

And so even as a very small child I dreaded growing up to be like the adults around me. I heard them saying too many cruel things about their dearest friends, saw too many of their false embraces with those they had just maligned, observed with horror their paranoic anger at some small slight or a fancied injury to their pride. They were, always, too unforgiving. In short, they did not have the careless magnanimity of children.

Sometimes there were problems for the daughters in the different customs between America and Italy. An Italian American woman from New York noted:

Our parents think you can just sit home and wait for a man to come asking for your hand—like a small town in Italy. They don't realize that here a girl has got to get out and do something about it.

The DiBrozzo family posed for this photograph in 1916. Samuele DiBrozzo (front row, third from left) went to Milwaukee in the 1890s, where he became a leader of the Italian American community. His son Aladino (back row, fifth from left) was one of the first Italian American lawyers in Milwaukee.

In 1942, a Brooklyn couple cherishes their new baby underneath a photograph of their wedding.

In most Italian families, daughters who worked were expected to bring home their pay envelopes unopened and turn them over to their mothers. Amalia Morandi's sister rebelled:

She used to open the envelope and take a few dollars if she needed it. They [her sister and friends] would have costume balls and she would come home at 12 o'clock—that was terrible, especially for the Italian people. That was awful, when a woman, a girl at her age, which was 18 or 19, when they came home at 12 o'clock the neighbors would gossip, would say look at that girl coming home by herself. My mother would talk to her, it did no good. It went in one ear and out the other. And then one day she came home and she says to my mother, she wanted to give her board. And my mother says whatdaya mean by board—my mother knew what she meant. She says, oh I give you so much a week and then the rest is for me. So my mother says all right, go ahead, do what you please.

In 1938, an older Italian American woman, Maria Frazaetti, expressed her feelings about old and new customs.

There are no old-country customs prevailing in our house. My children follow the American customs. I would like them to remember that the parents must be considered as an authority. I approve of allowing my children the freedom they desire; by doing so, they learn for themselves. My children misunderstand me when I advise them what style clothes they should wear. I blame styles and clothes on some of the stuff in magazines and the movies of this country. If I had

Alfonso Torre stands with his daughter Mildred and son Arthur in the doorway of his store in Paterson, New Jersey, in 1920. Alfonso's wife, Mary, looks out from behind the window.

Dinnertime was a family occasion in Italian American homes. The working father expected that his wife and children would greet him with a hearty meal on the table.

my way I would like my children to follow some of the old disciplinary laws of the old country.

The wedding of a daughter was a highlight in the life of an Italian family. Letitia Serpe recalled hers.

I got married in Mama's store. Mama went all out for my wedding. Even though we didn't have a lot of money, she gave me such a beautiful wedding. Everyone was there, the whole family, all the friends, practically the whole neighborhood. Mama gave me a beautiful trousseau...all kinds of beautiful linen that she embroidered herself. I still have some of it. Everybody ate, drank, and danced so much. It was so beautiful. If I close my eyes I can still see it in my mind. Mama gave me a beautiful day.

Pietro di Donato was one of the first Italian American novelists. He recalled that when he was a boy, his mother obtained a job for him with an Italian employer. She told Pietro's new boss:

I beg you, Signore Pellegrini, help me to save my first-born masculine from the savage manners of the braying Americans who consume parents, respect not Christians, nor revere the humility of gentle Christ. My son will obey you as keenly as the razor's edge.... Otherwise I'll ring his noggin like a bell.

The Bratta family of Chicago enjoys a picnic around 1939. The Italian immigrants brought their homeland's musical tradition with them to America. Many knew—and joyously played and sang—the music and lyrics of the great operas of Italian composers.

THE CHURCH

Theresa DiMarco on the day of her first Communion in 1927. This religious occasion was a rite of passage, marking when a child was able to receive the body of Christ at the Catholic mass.

Anthony Gisolfi and his brothers went to the local public school and received Catholic religious training in Sunday classes at their parish church.

As far back as I can remember—age four, perhaps—I was put to bed with the Sign of the Cross: *In nome del Padre, del Figliuolo, e dello Spiritu Santo. E cosi sia.*

The words were so inculcated that, when a little later on, in religious training at Sunday school, they became, In the name of the Father, the Son, and the Holy Ghost. Amen.

The earlier Italian was never forgotten.

Together with the Sign of the Cross...we repeated after Mother the *Pater Noster* and the *Ave Maria*

> *Padre nostro che sei nel cielo....*
>
> *Ave Maria, piena di grazia....*

And we also repeated after Mother another prayer, over and over again

> *Requiem aeternam dona eis, Domine....*

after being told we were reciting it for *il nonno* (grandfather) or *la nonna* (Father's mother) who were no longer in this world.... The quiet repetition of strange words, over and over, in the same rhythm, was a soothing prelude to sleep at that earliest age.

I could not have been more than six when I acquired the

Italian Americans paid particular devotion to the saints of their native Italy. Here, in a church named for Saint Dominic, worshipers have lighted candles before a shrine of another beloved Italian figure, Saint Francis of Assisi.

concept of *Paradiso*—Heaven—as the place to which all good people went, after some time, perhaps, in *Purgatorio*. Our prayers were to help them on their journey.

Soon afterwards—at age six—our formal religious instruction—in English, of course—was taken over by the nuns in Sunday School. There...we learned by rote, memorizing both Questions and Answers of the Catechism:

Who made the world?

Why did God make me?

I remember that I learned well, reciting when called on and not departing from the little text with the light blue cover distributed to each pupil....

By age seven the seriousness of receiving the Lord was impressed upon me. I was awed, and also made to doubt whether I was worthy of receiving the Lord, the Host, in Holy Communion—First Holy Communion. I was schooled in examining my conscience, to ask myself whether I had sinned, and if I had sinned, whether I was sorry. It was further impressed upon me that, if I committed a mortal sin and did not repent, I should be lost: I should not be united with God in heaven to love him and serve him, but should be condemned in all eternity.

A real concern and fear led me and other boys to examine our sins: lying, being disobedient, failing to say our prayers, fighting and hurting others. We were relieved to learn from Sister that these, for the most part, were "venial sins" and would not lose us for all eternity, but they had to be fully confessed.

Still, in my mind and in my heart I knew fear. Some nights, when...I did not fall asleep immediately, I would lie awake for hours, and actually be afraid of falling asleep a sinner. What sins had I committed, and was I really sorry for them?...

This fear did not, as I recall, lead me to Confession. I and my brothers always had to be reminded by Mother of our monthly obligation to go to Confession and receive Communion. And, still, from behind the screen of the confessional, I do not recall harsh or unkind words, I do not recall penances beyond five Our Fathers and five Hail Marys, I recall gently fatherly admonitions. Nor do I recall that sins were particularly hard to confess. Why the reluctance and why the fear? Perhaps...who knows...in a child as in the adult, there is a part of self that would remain inviolate....

Holy Week was particularly disturbing to me with its Forty Hours' Devotion. On Good Friday silence was maintained at home as well as in church. We were to speak, when necessary, in a low voice. We were not permitted to practice our piano lessons or play any games. Prayer, silent study, frugal eating marked the day. But the most disturbing element was the reiteration, in church and at home, that through our sins—my sins as well as those of others—we had brought about the horrors inflicted on Our Lord—the scourging, the Crucifixion, the piercing of His side.

A child loves a story, but there are some stories that frighten and disturb him. The physical horrors of the Passion

Anthony Gisolfi recalled the day of his First Holy Communion, when he and other seven-year-old children were permitted to receive the Host that Catholics believe is the Body of Christ:

We were prepared for First Holy Communion over what seemed to me a very long time with Sunday sessions and after-school sessions, and finally the day came. It was a late spring day—May or early June. Boys and girls stood in separate lines just outside the Church, before being led to occupy the forward pews.

My mother had attired me in a new blue suit with belted jacket and short trousers as became my age, soft white silk bow-tie, and white silk arm-band (as prescribed for the occasion), new low brown shoes, and new brown hose [stockings] that reached just below the knee....

I went in, in my proper place, knelt and prayed with all the other children. The girls all in white and wearing white veils occupied one side of the front pews; the boys all in blue and wearing flowing white bow-ties occupied the other. I received Holy Communion in my turn and was very careful to let the Host melt in my mouth before I swallowed it.

It was customary for an Italian American boy to wear a white ribbon on the sleeve of his new suit on the day of his first Communion. The ribbon symbolized the purity of his soul, for shortly before he had also made his first confession, absolving him of his sins.

affected me more than the peace of the Resurrection. I should have been a happier child, perhaps, if that had not been the case, but I can only record what I felt between the ages of eight and eleven or twelve.

Robert Orsi describes his experiences as an altar boy in a North Bronx Italian parish.

Our church was a Franciscan one and in all seasons the monks could be seen walking about the Bronx neighborhood in brown sandals and capes. Most of these men were Italian Americans, born in places like Jersey City and Union City, but some came from Italy.... These older monks fascinated me. My father told me stories about their special powers and histories; one was said to be an exorcist, another a visionary. They had names like Pacifica and Ludovico, and contact with them was mainly as their altar boy at very early morning Masses. They were rough with me, knuckling me in the head with hard, calloused knuckles, roughly adjusting my surplice, treating me in fact like a a beloved but intractable barnyard animal; they were also the ones to go and get me coffee and rolls in the mornings when I served the six o'clock mass....

The nuns who taught us were members of an Italian American order, brought especially to the neighborhood in the late 1940s by an Italian pastor, a smart and experienced man, who had no intention of having his people's children exposed to the prejudices of Irish American nuns. That is not to say that our nuns were without prejudices. They were tough women, rough and determined in their labor of shaping the matters that came into their thick hands.

Italian Americans celebrate March 19, the Feast of San Giuseppe (Saint Joseph), with as much devotion as Irish Americans celebrate St. Patrick's Day. Here, in 1930, the children of All Saints Church in Chicago prepare for the annual St. Joseph's Day Procession.

Fabbia Orzo remembered why her mother had a particular devotion to St. Anthony.

St. Anthony was her favorite saint and she had reasons to believe in St. Anthony. My mother was crippled before her youngest son was born. She couldn't walk. Three months after she gave birth she couldn't walk until she prayed to St. Anthony. One day a parade for St. Anthony went past her window. My mother prayed that she be able to walk to the window and see the parade for St. Anthony walk by. She said if this happened she would go to church no matter where it was to pray for the saint, and pay her respects. She did walk those few steps to the window and from then on she regained her health.

For many Italians, the Roman Catholic church was not a refuge, for it was controlled by the Irish clergy. Jerre Mangione describes an incident in Rochester:

Generally, there was little communication between my relatives and the non-Italian world. Nowhere was this more evident than at St. Bridget, a nearby Catholic Church where most of my relatives worshipped. The parish priest was a short-tempered Irishman, who deeply resented the fact that most of his congregation now consisted of Italians, many of whom did not understand a word he said. His fierce demands from the pulpit for contributions were often mistaken by the Italians as diatribes against the devil. My brother and I deplored his obvious dislike of the Sicilians in his congregation, particularly in his habit of bullying them for not contributing enough money for the support of the church. One Sunday morning, while the priest was passing the collection plate, we witnessed a scene that caused my eleven-year-old brother to explode. When the priest reached the pew in front of us, a poor Sicilian widow we knew dropped a nickel into the collection basket only to have it thrown back in her face. Before I could stop him, my brother was on his feet shouting at the priest: "You can't do that. She's poor. She can't afford any more." The priest was too stunned to say anything. My brother was trembling, frightened by his impulsive action. I took him by the hand (I am sixteen months older) and we made a hasty exit.

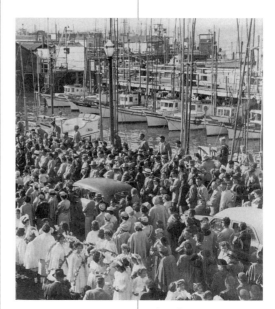

Like other Roman Catholics, Italian Americans ask priests to give the church's blessing to important occasions. Here, around the year 1940, is the annual blessing of the fleet at Fisherman's Wharf in San Francisco.

SCHOOL

As a girl proudly holds the flag, students say the Pledge of Allegiance at the Mott Street School in New York's Little Italy in 1892. In both public and Catholic schools, the children of immigrants learned the history and patriotic values of their new country.

A beginner's English class in 1912 at the Detroit Street Social Center in the Italian neighborhood of Milwaukee, Wisconsin. Many of the adult students probably came from a long day at work, but they felt that learning English would help them find better jobs.

Angelo Pellegrini, who came to America in 1913, related his experiences in an American school in McCleary, Washington.

One day in hygiene class we were discussing the care of the teeth....Everyone talked glibly of visits to the dentist, of a certain number of cavities filled, of the excruciating pain bravely endured in the dentist's chair, etc. What did Angelo have to report? Nothing. Absolutely nothing. I had never heard of a dentist up to that day.... I felt very much embarrassed—an alien, an inferior breed who had never had what everybody could boast of: a tooth cavity drilled and filled by a dentist.

For a brief while I felt like an oddity. And then, quite unexpectedly, I became a hero. The teacher asked me if I would let her look at my teeth....When she had completed the examination she announced to the class with considerable and undisguised excitement that she had seen a miracle: a perfect set of teeth.

Constantine Panunzio won a scholarship to a private high school, where he was the only Italian student. He found that even the teachers had certain misconceptions about what Italians were like. One day, Panunzio recalled, a male teacher asked him to stay after class. The teacher told him solemnly, "In this country, it is not customary to carry knives." Panunzio remembered:

He used the word "stiletto" synonymously with the word "knife." There appeared to be some uncertainty in his mind as to just what it was but one thing was certain: I had a weapon and I was an Italian. That was enough. All Italians carry weapons and are dangerous creatures, according to the common American belief. He assured me that he harbored no ill feelings toward me, but he made it plain that it was not a good thing to carry a weapon and that since coming to the school I had caused great disturbance by openly carrying a "stiletto."..."Unless you give it up," he continued, "you will be obliged to leave school."

Finally...to clinch the matter, [he] said that he himself had seen it a few moments before, and for that reason he asked me to remain. If I did not mind, he would at least like to look at it. The point of it was even then to be seen sticking out of my vest pocket, shining brightly against a blue silk handkerchief. I could deny it no longer. Taking hold of the lapel of my coat, he pulled it open, reached for the dreaded weapon and pulled it out...

It was an *aluminum comb*, conveniently pointed at one end to be used for manicuring, and not for carving out human hearts! It did look very much like a stiletto.... To this day, I venture to say, some of my schoolmates still remember the dreadful days when they went to school with an Italian who carried a stiletto with which he intended to carve out hearts, both men's and maidens'!

Later, when Panunzio became a social worker, he saw the other side of the coin, discovering why many Italian American families feared sending their children to "an American school."

A woman in our constituency had three children, two boys, one seven and the other five years old, and a baby girl. She was a widow and was having a bitter struggle to eke out an existence. She came to me one day requesting that I interest myself in placing the little girl in a nursery, and the boys in a kindergarten or school. I proceeded to make such arrangements at the public school, when one day she came to my office and broke out crying. I could not make out what the trouble was. After she calmed down...she finally said, "Please don't send my children to an *American school*, for as soon as they learn English they will not be my children anymore. I know many children who as soon as they learn English become estranged from their parents. I want to send my babies to a school where they can be taught in the Italian language."

Some Italian families sent their sons, but not daughters, for education beyond high school. A woman identified only as Lily explained the reasons for this.

I came to America with my mother when I was four years old. My father was here first. He came here in 1912. We came in 1913. My mother, my brother and I. We didn't speak a word of English. We had to learn to speak English. We went to grammar school in Bayonne [New Jersey]....

My only problem was that while in America my mother had a new baby every two years. And I had to stay home to help take care of the babies, so that my mother could scrub clothes by hand. I missed a lot of school. And I had a lot of trouble learning. Missing two or three days a week of school, I couldn't catch up with the work. In those days, they didn't believe a girl needed an education, because she got married and became a mother and a housewife. All my brothers got an education and so did my two younger sisters. They graduated from high school. Those days high school was enough....They all got good jobs, being high school graduates.

I went to work as a seamstress when I was 14 to help educate my brothers and sisters. I worked in a factory...until I was 22, when I got married. The burden of helping the family fell on my shoulders because I was the oldest. My brother went to the University of Maryland and became a dentist. Since I was the oldest of the girls, there was no education for me. I got as far as the ninth grade and then I had to go to work.

The cover of this textbook, used by Italian American children in a public school in 1943, shows Uncle Sam with children of different immigrant groups. The ideals of the time stressed America's role as a "melting pot" in which the children and grandchildren of immigrants blended in with the rest of the population.

One Italian showed me a letter that he said had
secured him several jobs. It was from an
alderman in the Nineteenth Ward of Chicago
whose reign has been long and notorious. It read:
"This is a neighbor and a friend of mine. Please
give him work." And long after the man has
passed from the group of laborers who are
dependent upon casual and irregular work and
has become the prosperous owner of a grocery
store, he will remember his "neighbor and
friend" and be glad to do for him any small favor
that he can. The only favors asked of him will be
at election time, and in his gratitude the Italian
will in all probability vote against his own and the
city's interest.

SOCIAL CLUBS AND ASSOCIATIONS

The Sons of Italy, founded in 1905, was the first national Italian American organization. Its charter gives an idea of its ideals and goals, and also reflects its founders' awareness of the prejudice against Italian Americans.

We, the members of the Order Sons of Italy in America, a fraternal organization, being a part of the United States of America, which we serve at all times with undivided devotion, and to whose progress we dedicate ourselves; united in the belief in God; conscious of being a representative element of an old civilization which has contributed to the enlightenment of the human spirit, and which through our activities, institutions, and customs may enrich and broaden the pattern of the American way of life; realizing that through an intelligent and constant exercise of civic duties and rights, and obedience to the Constitution of the United States, we uphold and strengthen this republic...the said Order Sons of Italy in America do hereby ordain and establish the following as our constitution:

The purposes of the order are:

(a) to enroll in its membership all persons of Italian birth or descent, regardless of religious faith or political affiliation, who believe in the fundamental concept that society is based upon principles of law and order, and who adhere to a form of government founded upon the belief in God and based upon the Constitution of the United States of America...;

(b) to promote civic education among its members;

(c) to uphold the concept of Americanism;

(d) to encourage the dissemination of Italian culture in the United States;

(e) to keep alive the spiritual attachment to the traditions of the land of our ancestors;

(f) to promote the moral, intellectual, and material well-being of our membership;

(g) to defend and uphold the prestige of the people of Italian birth or descent in America;

(h) to encourage the active participation of our membership in the political, social, and civic life of our communities;

(i) to organize and establish benevolent and social welfare institutions for the protection and assistance of our members, their dependents, and the needy in general, with such material aid as we are able to give.

Italians, like other groups, learned how to obtain patronage jobs from the local political organization. For some, this was the most important reason for becoming citizens. In the 1970s, one old woman recalled:

I never made myself a citizen. I don't know how to read and write, so what was the sense. My husband became a citizen. Through his club, it happened—you know—the Society. At election time he found himself there with people who knew how to make citizens, and so, I don't know how, I don't know why, but they used to call him all the time when elections were held. It helped the Italians, he told me—those elections. If it weren't for them, my husband couldn't be sure of a job all the time.

The prominente *were leaders of the Italian business community and social clubs. Sometimes they acted as representatives of the Italian community in dealings with the city government. In 1904, an Italian journalist described a typical leader.*

He may have first worked as a laborer himself and somehow been able to save enough money to establish himself and his family in the United States. He boasts of friendship with many important Americans, though they are probably lower-level Irish and Jewish politicians and professionals.... He is president or treasurer of various Italian societies, is invariably an American citizen and is usually politically active, directing his clients' votes toward the party from whom he can expect the greatest favors. He goes from Republican to Democrat, offering a block of 20,000 votes, which are usually no more than 1,000. After determining the source of his greatest gain, he persuades those eligible to vote to follow his example.

The members of the Young Men's Lincoln Club of Little Italy celebrate Lincoln's Birthday in 1915. Patriotic displays demonstrated the loyalty of Italian immigrants to their adopted country.

An Italian Club picnic in Thurber, Texas, early in the 20th century. The club's flag is modeled after the national flag of Italy. Wherever Italian immigrants settled, they kept their traditions and customs alive in gatherings like this.

Often, Italian immigrants returned home for visits after they had become prosperous. There, they found that both they and their homeland had changed. Such people were called trapiantati—*"transplanted persons." As one wrote, he felt truly at home neither in the old country nor the new:*

You see my friend, you come back to your own land after almost forty years, and how do they treat you? Like a dog. They almost tell you you're not Italian any more. And over there they tell you you're not American. So you are nothing. Believe me, if you leave your country for more than five years, you're lost. You don't belong anywhere.

But another immigrant returning home felt a sense of joy in his new identity. When Anthony Mancini stood before the house where his father had been born:

I didn't cry. My heart didn't beat faster. But I was very glad I came. For the house, like the town and even Italy in general, confirmed my suspicions. I wasn't underneath *really* Italian. Neither was I just another good old red-blooded American. I was an Italian-American—a unique breed, an identity in itself.

In 1909, an earthquake devastated parts of Sicily. Italian Americans responded with aid for the victims, many of whom were friends and relatives. In New York's Little Italy, people throw contributions from their tenement windows into collection wagons in the street.

TIES TO THE HOMELAND

As the following letters from immigrants indicate, many Italian Americans kept close ties to their families back home in Italy.

My dear father,
...you want my photo very much but for now I am not able to satisfy you because the reason is this— that where I am at work there are no photographers because I am a little far away from the city. However in another letter I will make you happy.

Dear brother now I want to talk to you a bit. Well, you tell me that there has been a lot of hail in our fields and so you tell me you want to come to America because in Italy you can't get ahead any more.... I would be ready to send you the ticket but after I had arranged for you to come here what you make would not be enough to eat this winter....

And so dear brother please listen a little to what I say. For now, hoe the fields and...so the work you do this winter will all be to the advantage of our home.... If you want to get married do so at your convenience because I [will] send you a little money very soon...

Dear wife,
I come to you with these few lines to let you know about the excellent state of my health...and [in an earlier letter] you tell me that you all are feeling good and you dear wife tell me about your pregnancy. You tell me that it is going along well and I am very pleased...and I pray God night and day for you to have courage for when you will give birth God willing. Please take care of yourself and do not [worry] so much about me for if I were a bird I would fly to Italy when you give birth but please do not be frightened for God willing there will come a day when we will embrace again. Pray to God that he may give you both strength and good luck for I dear wife think of you always night and day.

During World War I, the United States and Italy were allies. Visiting Italy after the war broke out, Constantine Panunzio saw the flags of his homeland and his adopted country flying side by side. He described his feelings.

Before my eyes the two national standards...were waving triumphantly in the stiff breeze sweeping over the mountain crest. One stood for Italy, both ancient and modern, which the world respects; for the Italy of my childhood, for all the memories of my youth, of loved ones, for all that had been beautiful and lovely in my boyhood; for the tender memories of loved ones, living and dead. The other stood for all the suffering of the years, for the awakening of manhood, for the birth of freedom, for the unfolding of life. I loved not one the less, but the other more!

Attilio Piccirilli, a sculptor, described his sense of being deeply rooted in America to an interviewer in 1938.

I have been an American for so long—fifty years—that I often forget I was born in Italy. When anyone refers to me as a foreigner, or as an Italian, I pretend that I haven't heard and I don't usually answer. Of course, I am an American.... Once I went back to my native city and planned to stay there for a year or more. I locked the door of my studio in New York, said good-bye to all my friends and went to the homeland where I had been born. What did I find? I was a foreigner in Italy. I could speak the language of course, but I couldn't think Italian.... I had planned to be away for a year but in four months I was on my return trip to the Bronx....

I first *knew* that I was a real American when I brought my mother's body back from Italy where she had died on a visit. We buried her here and I made a statue of motherhood for her grave. I had worked here and succeeded a little, and taken an oath of allegiance. But it is when you bury one you love in a country's soil that you realize that you belong to that soil forever.

After Benito Mussolini came to power in Italy in the 1920s, he established a fascist dictatorship, jailing or killing his political opponents. Among those who fled Mussolini's tyranny was journalist Max Ascoli. Ascoli arrived in 1931; later he eloquently described his feelings on applying for American citizenship.

It is a very strange thing to acquire the citizenship of a new country: something like taking a new father and mother. There is no doubt that the natural destiny of every man is to live and die in the land where he was born, among the people of his own language and tradition and customs. How strange it would have sounded to me if, only a dozen years ago, I would have been told that one day I might give up being an Italian!...

I don't regret it. I would do it again. I could not become a Fascist. I became an American. Therefore Italy is my former country. The Italian culture is my former culture....

I am told to go with my witnesses into a bare courtroom. A thin elderly man in shirt sleeves, sitting on the bench, calls my name. At his side is the American flag. On the grayed walls are two cheap old pictures, one of Washington and the other of Lincoln....

I become an American citizen. So help me God.

Enrico Fermi

Of the many Italians who fled the fascist regime of Benito Mussolini, none helped his adopted country more than the scientific genius Enrico Fermi. Born in Rome in 1901, Fermi built an electric motor when he was still a boy. As a student at the University of Pisa, his great gifts were so obvious that one day a professor asked him to lecture to the class on Albert Einstein's theory of relativity, which the professor himself did not understand.

Fermi continued his research into the mystery of the atom. In 1938, Fermi won the Nobel Prize for physics. This award came at a fortunate time, for Mussolini, like his Nazi ally, Adolf Hitler, had just passed anti-Jewish legislation. Laura, Enrico's wife, was Jewish. After accepting the prize, Fermi brought his wife and two children to the United States.

As war loomed in Europe, Fermi taught at Columbia University in New York City. Hearing that German scientists were trying to split the atom, Fermi set to work with the same goal in mind. His research in Italy had shown that if neutrons, part of the nucleus of the atom, were bombarded by the particles of certain elements, the atom could be split, releasing enormous amounts of energy. If the process could be controlled, a weapon with greater power than ever before might be created.

After Pearl Harbor, Fermi's friend Albert Einstein wrote President Franklin Roosevelt, urging him to support Fermi's research. Roosevelt agreed, and the United States began a race with Germany to develop the first atomic bomb. On December 2, 1942, at the University of Chicago, Fermi supervised the first nuclear chain reaction that made the construction of a bomb possible. The U.S. government science adviser to the top-secret project telegraphed news of the success to President Roosevelt with the code phrase: "The Italian navigator has landed in the New World."

After World War II, Enrico Fermi received the Congressional Medal of Merit, the highest civilian honor bestowed by the United States government. He continued his work and was further honored when a group of scientists who discovered chemical element 100 named it Fermium, after him. Tragically, like many others who worked with radioactive elements, he developed cancer. Fermi died in 1954.

June 10, 1940, was a significant day for all Italian Americans. Benito Mussolini, the fascist dictator of Italy, declared war on France and England, making Italy an ally of Nazi Germany. Though the United States was then still a neutral country, it seemed clear that it would soon be drawn into the war in Europe. Italian Americans realized that their fellow citizens suspiciously wondered where their loyalties lay. A son of Italian immigrants described the feelings in New York's Little Italy.

Outdoors on our block, the reaction to the news...was a curious, but only seeming calm, as I returned home from work early in the evening. Everybody was unusually quiet. I missed the shouting and laughter of children on the sidewalks, the cries of boys playing stick ball in the street. The neighborhood iceman sat on the shoe repairer's doorstep, but they were not arguing as is their custom. Men and women in front of stores and tenements looked about almost furtively, as though they were suddenly being watched. Down the street a group of men stood in front of the grocer's. Their discussion was subdued....I know most of them; nearly all are immigrants who came over shortly before or after the First World War. A small proportion of them are pro-Fascist, but they really express themselves only in the privacy of their homes....

I spent an hour last night in the corner candy store where a bunch of young fellows hang out. I caught phrases: "Ford says he can make a thousand planes a day.... La Guardia is a wop,

Though the United States and Italy were enemies in World War II, Italian Americans overwhelmingly supported their adopted country. Rose Carrendeno displays the framed card that indicates three of her sons were serving in the armed forces of the United States.

In 1942, patriotic banners fly over Mott Street in New York's Little Italy and people crowd onto the fire escapes to cheer a passing parade.

too, ain't he?.... Did you hear what Roosevelt said about Musso? The sonoffa—" meaning the latter.

There is a boy in our block who spends a lot of his free time in the branch library. He has read up on Italy. A year ago he dreamed of going over some day for a visit. He wanted to see Florence. Now that's out. Last night I met him in front of the library as it closed at ten. I asked him, "How do you feel about all this?"

He said, "Mussolini's action puts me in position where I am obliged to fight my own mother."

Author Gay Talese describes the divided loyalty that Italian Americans faced during World War II in a book about his father, Joseph, who was an immigrant from southern Italy.

Roosevelt's declaration of war against Japan after the latter's surprise air attack on the American naval base at Pearl Harbor, on December 7, 1941, meant that Japan's Axis allies, Italy and Germany, were obliged to take sides against the United States; and thus Americans of Italian descent were now officially at war with their families in Italy. Joseph's situation was typical: while he was parading his patriotism by volunteering for patrol duty along the boardwalk with other members of his Rotary Club, his brothers and other relatives overseas were dressed in Fascist uniforms strutting to the goose step that Mussolini had introduced in the hope that his soldiers might look and act more like the bellicose Nazi troops whom the Duce envied and revered.

[By the end of 1944, the airplanes of the United States and its allies were bombing southern Italy. While Joseph's relatives in his home town, Maida, carried a statue of St. Francis through the streets, Joseph himself, in Ocean City, New Jersey, prayed to the same saint.]

Throughout the winter of 1944, Joseph prayed several times each day in the living room of his home, kneeling on the red velvet of the prie-dieu under the portrait of the saint, ignoring the store bell below and leaving the operation of his business largely to his wife.... A high percentage of the clientele now were American servicemen on shore leave...and among such customers, many of whom had returned from triumphant tours in Sicily and Italy, Joseph could not always conceal the humiliation and divided loyalty he felt as an emotional double agent....

Joseph continued to keep up with the war news in the daily press, but now he bought the papers at a newsstand beyond the business district, a six-block trip instead of the short walk to the corner cigar store, because he wanted to avoid the neighborhood merchants and his other acquaintances who lingered there.... The last time he had gone there,...Mussolini had dominated the headlines (he had just been imprisoned by the Italian king) and as Joseph left with his papers underarm, he heard a familiar voice calling out from the rear of the store: "Hey, Joe, what's gonna happen to your friend now?"

John Basilone

One of the greatest American heroes of the Second World War was Sergeant John Basilone. The son of Italian immigrants, Basilone joined the Marines and soon after Pearl Harbor sailed with his unit to the Pacific island of Guadalcanal. A battle raged between American and Japanese troops for control of the island. For three days and nights in October 1942, Basilone held off a whole regiment of Japanese soldiers with a machine gun. During this time, he stopped neither for food nor sleep. Time after time, the Japanese launched assaults, only to be mowed down by Basilone's fire. He moved only when the pile of Japanese bodies grew so high that it blocked his line of fire. General Douglas MacArthur called him a "one-man army" for his heroics. He was the first Marine to win the Congressional Medal of Honor in World War II.

After receiving the medal, John Basilone returned to his hometown of Raritan, New Jersey. As a war hero, his arrival was greeted with a parade, flowers and speeches. The Navy Department assigned Basilone to train Marines. He also participated in War Bond Drives. But he could only think of the his companions back in the Pacific and asked to be returned to combat. He died in the assault on Iwo Jima in 1945. Posthumously he received the Navy Cross.

The Sciorra family of Brooklyn, New York, in 1981. Everything on the table was baked by Mrs. Sciorra.

CHAPTER SIX

A PART OF AMERICA

orld War II was a turning point in the history of Italian Americans. About one million Italian Americans served in the military forces of the United States; fighting side by side with other Americans, they broke down the stereotypes that had plagued their parents. War heroes such as Sergeant John Basilone exemplified the courage that had marked the struggle of the older generation of immigrants.

During the war, Congress passed the G.I. Bill, which provided tuition for veterans to go to college, and low-interest loans so that they could purchase houses and businesses. Italian Americans took advantage of the opportunity, as did many other Americans. As one recalled, "The G.I. Bill gave many of our men the economic ladder to go up and the FHA [Federal Housing Authority, which administered the loans] gave them the money to get out [of slums]."

The G.I. Bill made possible the postwar movement of Americans out of crowded urban areas and into the suburbs. Second- and third-generation Italian Americans, whose fathers and grandfathers had been "pickashovel" men,

started construction businesses that prospered from the house-building boom. At the same time, many younger Italian Americans left the Little Italys of the inner cities for new suburban homes.

In the postwar period, more Italian Americans attended college, learning the skills that brought them prominence in business. Lee Iacocca, later the head of the Chrysler Corporation, was one of them. The children and grandchildren of immigrant laborers became doctors, lawyers, poets, novelists, teachers, and movie directors. Italian Americans have won awards that range from Nobel Prizes to Oscars.

This very success, however, pulled some of them away from the traditions that had been the guiding force of their families. Even those Italian Americans who attained the American dream of material success often felt a sense of conflict at losing their roots. Some realized that in the process they had lost something valuable. In the 1980s, a young Italian American in New York told an interviewer: "The only time I really felt close to my grandfather was when he drove me past a post office in Brooklyn. He had to stop the car and get out and explain how he helped build it.... He was so happy, so thrilled to be part of

it. It was like it meant more to him than anything else he had ever done. And maybe he's right. There it was, forty years after he worked on it, and it still looked good. He did a good job—anybody could see that. I doubt I will ever be able to point something like that out to my grandchildren—forty years after I do it—so they and everybody else can look at it and say, 'Whoever did that did a really good job.'"

Some traditions have survived to become major celebrations. In many towns and cities, the little religious festivals that generations of Italian immigrants held as reminders of their homeland and religious culture have continued to the present day. Now, many of them last a week or two, and Americans of all ethnic backgrounds and faiths come to enjoy the music, the food, and the fun. The San Gennaro festival in New York's Little Italy is famous as one of the oldest of these *festas*.

In recent decades, Italian Americans have created their own festas, celebrations of *la via nuova*. The largest of these takes place over four days in mid-July in Milwaukee, Wisconsin. Festa Italiana, as it is called, attracts hundreds of thousands of people from all over the midwestern states. Everyone who attends, regardless of their origin, celebrates the Italian American heritage in America.

In becoming part of mainstream America, Italian Americans also found that one stereotype continued to plague them. That was the image of the Mafia. From the 19th century onward, Italian Americans were suspected of having something to do with an organized criminal gang. That was the charge that led a New Orleans mob to lynch 11 Italians in 1891. More than a century later, in 1992, the same rumor of Mafia connections helped to defeat New York's Geraldine Ferraro in her campaign for the U.S. Senate. The word *Mafia* has been a slur hurled at all Italian Americans.

There was, and is, a Mafia criminal organization in Sicily. But there is little connection between it and the small number of Italian Americans who have become involved in organized crime in the United States. Yet sensational accounts in the mainstream press have made the American "Mafia" seem like a much larger organization than it is.

The best-known Italian American criminal, Al Capone, was a Brooklyn-born bootlegger and thug who headed a Chicago-based criminal organization in the 1920s and 1930s. Though Capone never belonged to any nationwide Mafia conspiracy, his flamboyance and success—

achieved with the cooperation of corrupt, non-Italian city officials—added to the myth of the Italian criminal. Today's Italian Americans deeply resent the popular perception that the Mafia is part of their heritage.

On the other hand, Italian

In the bicentennial year 1976, Pietro Carolfi works on a plaster mold for a statue of The Signer *that now stands in Independence Park, Philadelphia.*

Americans have taken pride in their many *compari* who have received popular acclaim in the worlds of entertainment and sports. Italian American neighborhoods often had theaters where popular immigrant entertainers appeared. The most famous called

himself Farfariello (Little Butterfly). The first Italian immigrant to gain nationwide fame was Rudolph Valentino. Born Rodolfo Guglielmi in southern Italy, he came to New York City in 1913, taking work as a dishwasher, a janitor, and a gardener. His talent as a tango dancer, however, won him a Hollywood contract. He made only three movies, but they created the image of the dark, passionate Latin lover.

Valentino has been followed by a long line of Italian American motion picture stars, many of whom adopted his intense, hot-blooded screen image. Among the most famous are Oscar winners Al Pacino and Robert De Niro, as well as Sylvester Stallone, who not only starred in the widely popular *Rocky* and *Rambo* films, but wrote them as well. Popular Italian American actresses have included Anne Bancroft (Anna Maria Italiano), Annette Funicello, and TV soap-opera favorite Susan Lucci.

Another immigrant, Frank (Francesco) Capra, became one of Hollywood's greatest directors during the 1930s and 1940s. In films such as *Mr. Smith Goes to Washington*, Capra created his own vision of America—a place where the "little guy" always triumphed, where love, family, and honesty were more important than money. It was a powerful message in depression-era America, and audiences flocked to Capra's movies, not knowing that his films reflected the values of his native Sicily.

Today's Italian American movie directors—such as Michael Cimino, Francis Ford Coppola, and Martin Scorsese—have made films with darker, more serious themes, sometimes drawing on their youthful experiences in Italian American urban neighborhoods.

In their homeland, Italians have a long musical tradition, which they brought with them to America. Music halls, with everything from popular songs to opera, were favorite gathering places for the Italian immigrants. The single most famous Italian American entertainer, Frank Sinatra, developed his style of singing from listening to Italian American radio stars Carlo Butto and Russ Columbo. The list of outstanding Italian American singers is very long, ranging from legendary opera singers Adelina Patti and Rosa Ponselle to rock stars Dion and Madonna—both of whom dropped their last names, DiMucci and Ciccone, respectively.

Italian Americans have also made their way into the national spotlight in sports. The Italian American community cheered in 1911 when Ping Bodie (born Pezzolo) first took the field for the Chicago White Sox. As many others with Italian names entered the major leagues, Italian Americans felt a greater sense that they were becoming part of America. A boy in Boston, Angelo Bartlett Giamatti—who would one day be commissioner of baseball—made

up an all-Italian team, which included Yogi Berra, Phil Rizzuto, Tony Lazzeri, and two of the three DiMaggio brothers (Dom and Joe). The manager of such a team today would have to be either Tommy Lasorda or Tony LaRussa, both of whom led teams to World Series wins.

The Italian American Sports Hall of Fame also includes the only undefeated heavyweight boxing champion, Rocky Marciano, racecar driver Mario Andretti, golfer Gene Sarazen, and countless football players from Frank Carideo to Joe Montana, who led his team to two Super Bowl victories. Football coach Vince Lombardi became famous for his slogan, "Winning isn't everything: it's the only thing."

That philosophy also applies to politics, and since the late 19th

A group of Italian American men compete on a Philadelphia bocce court in 1982. Bocce is one of the games that Italian immigrants brought to the New World.

century Italian Americans have won the respect, and votes, of their fellow citizens in seeking public office. Probably the best-loved Italian American politician was the colorful Fiorello La Guardia, who served New York both as congressman and mayor between 1916 and

1945. John Pastore of Rhode Island was both the first Italian American elected governor of a state (in 1946) and the first to take a seat in the U.S. Senate (in 1950). Geraldine Ferraro scored two firsts when she received the Democratic party nomination for Vice President in 1984. Though she lost, she was the first woman of a major party and the first Italian American ever to run for that office. Today, an Italian American (Antonin Scalia) sits on the Supreme Court for the first time; many others serve as mayors, governors, representatives, and senators. The day seems not far off when the President of the United States will have a name "that ends in a vowel"—an Italian name.

Italian Americans have excelled in virtually every area of American life. But the most pervasive sign that they have truly become part of America is the popularity of Italian food. Is there any town, however small, without a pizza parlor? Is there any supermarket where spaghetti and macaroni are not on sale, both dried and in cans?

It was not always so. At the beginning of the 20th century, social workers named "eating macaroni" as one of the signs that Italian immigrants had not yet become "true Americans." But rather than abandon the delicious food of their homeland, Italian Americans opened their arms (and restaurants) and generously offered the rest of America this great gift. It is only one of many Italian American contributions to American culture.

CHANGING TIMES, CHANGING TRADITIONS

Between 1975 and 1988, three generations of Italian American women related their life stories to an interviewer. From grandmother to granddaughter, a traditional, strict, male-dominated upbringing shaped their lives. Yet, as the grandmother wrote, "times change," and each woman won a bit more independence.

Michelina Gaetano was born in Italy in 1890. When she was fifteen, her father arranged for her to marry Vincent Profeta, a man from their village who had emigrated to the United States.

I didn't know who [Profeta] was. He said he knew me. He remembered me because my hair was wavy, and [in Italy] he saw me making spaghetti with the hand and he liked the way I moved my hand, and he came to my grandmother's house all the time. [That was when] I was nine years and he was eighteen. How could I look at him? I didn't remember him at all.

I came [to the United States] the Fourth of July and married the last Sunday in July, the thirty-first of July, 1905. I came; I was twenty-seven days engaged and got married....

My husband was a very nice man. He would buy me lot of things—lavalieres, bracelet, ring, everything. But he had a little bit fast temper. I kept quiet, not because I was scared, because I was used to this in my country. Nobody was afraid, because he was never bad with the children. He was a very good father. I talked to him about the children and he always fixed it up. He would not make a fight. Yes, my husband was very nice with the children. He didn't play very much, because people from the old country have to act stuck-up, not play.

[The Profetas had four children; the eldest was Josephine, born in 1906.] Josephine finished grade school and went to high school two years. All the time they asked her to go swimming [in gym class] and put on a swimsuit. I did not like her to put on a swimsuit; her father would not allow her to put on a swimsuit and go in the water. She was ashamed to tell this to her girlfriends. She couldn't go swim; she would not go to school. So she quit.

I was glad she didn't go. I was glad she started work in Kaufmann's warehouse. My son Joe, he didn't want to finish high school. Joe was a smart boy and I wanted him to be a lawyer. He told me he didn't want to go to school anymore, and I took a big knife and said, "I put this in your chest if you don't go to school." Honest to God, I put it in the wall!...

I wanted my daughters to marry and be happy, that's all. Josephine was not allowed to go out with a boy [alone]. I had to go. My husband and I would go out with them, but with the second girl, Lucy [six years younger], no. She would go out

One immigrant's life story: In 1905, Dominic Justave arrived in his mother's arms (top) at Ellis Island, where an official changed the family name from Gustozzo. Dominic married Rose Carloni (center) in the 1920s. On Easter Sunday 1954, Dominic and Rose posed with their children and grandchildren at their Philadelphia home.

with the boyfriend [by herself]. Times change.... When my daughter Josephine was going with her [future] husband, my husband used to say to him, "when I'm not home and when my wife not home, you no stay here with my daughter." When [the boyfriend] was in the house, I watched from the dining room and the hall. I watched what he did, and my mother-in-law said to me, "You bad. Leave go the kids what they want to do. He just going to kiss her." But I watched. Till they got married, I watched.

Michelina Profeta's daughter Josephine recalled that as a young woman in the 1920s, she agreed with her parents' strict views.

When I was working...I'd get together with the girls for lunch. One time I told my parents I'd go to a movie after work, so they said, "All right." My girlfriend brought two fellows with her, one for herself and one for me. I said, "No, I don't think I'll go; I think I'll go home." My parents asked, "What happened?" and I told them, "The other girl brought a boy over and I thought maybe you wouldn't want me to go." That was it. That was the way I felt about it. I really followed what they suggested, because it wasn't that they really restricted [her from doing what she wanted to do]. What they restricted was what I believed in. That was the way it should be and that was the way it was.

[Josephine started going with the young man who would become her husband.] Of course, we were accompanied by my parents.... If we went to the movies, we would take them to the movies. If we went to visit friends, they'd come along. If we went for a walk, they would walk ten paces behind, but I mean

Four generations of an extended Italian American family in Pueblo, Colorado, in the 1980s. The framed pictures depict relatives who have died or were unable to join the family re-union.

The Grucci family of Brooklyn, New York, operates what is probably the best-known fireworks business in the United States. The Gruccis' elaborate displays have lit up the skies for many U.S. holidays.

they were there! And that was the way it should be, because we all did the same thing on that street [where the families were all Italian]. It wasn't as if I was tempted by seeing another person do something else.

Josephine's husband Joseph Fastuca tried to raise their own children the same way. But Josephine's ideas had changed:

M[y husband] was a little more strict than I was, because he came from Italy when he was sixteen or seventeen years old, and he never left any of that behind him. He sort of held onto their traditions....And me, I was a little different. I was born here and grew up here, and felt the difference that I didn't want my children to go through the same thing. So I would interfere sometimes.

One time, when [her eldest daughter] Joanna wanted to start to date—oh, she was about twenty-one, and he was still making a fuss that she couldn't go out. I said, "Look, don't fuss about it. She has to get out with someone, because if she doesn't how is she going to find someone to marry? They don't come to your doorstep today like they did before." Right! The first time she wanted to [drive to Chicago] she was going with two girlfriends in a car, and he wanted us to follow her with our car until she got to her destination. I had to fight that a little bit. I said, "No!" and said how ridiculous she would feel with her friends. And so he gave in....

Life is different for my children. Today parents have to bend a little to keep their children in line, because if they don't, they may lose them altogether....When we went [to her son's house] for Mother's Day dinner, my son said, "You know, I'm ashamed to see the kids walk in." They are not that bad. It's just that their hair is a little long. It bothers him, but he doesn't put his foot down. He sort of goes along with it, but he doesn't like it. That's the difference. We used to put our foot down, and that was it. Today it's a little different. I told him, "Don't worry about it. They will grow out of it."

Josephine Fastuca's daughter Joanna, born in 1931, was more resentful of her strict upbringing than her own mother had been. She felt that her parents treated her, their only daughter, differently from her three brothers.

There was definitely the idea that a girl is different than a boy, and I remember many times being upset about something and my mother would say, "Well, remember now, they're boys and you are a girl, and they can do things that you are not allowed to do." This used to make me so angry because I never could understand what difference it made, but these were the rules....

When I was in high school, I wasn't even allowed to go ice skating or roller skating, because boys where there and you just didn't go where boys were. I remember I had to go to the movies with my parents, and even in the movies it was always very funny, because my father always made sure that I sat between him and my mother. At sixteen, when you are still going to the movies with your parents, it can be a little bit embarrassing, but this is the way he wanted it and this is how we did it....

I was afraid to think of going against his wishes. I will tell you why I was afraid to. My cousins would sneak behind their parents' back and meet fellows on the side, and they were caught. I remember a friend of the family saw one girl with a boy and told the parents....I remember walking in and finding my father, my mother, my uncle, and my two aunts sitting in the living room and my cousin standing in the center of the living room. It was like the Inquisition: "What were you doing? Where were you? Where did you meet him? Why did you go behind our backs?" They were all so involved in this discipline, and I think that so frightened me that I did not dare go against their wishes.

[When Joanna was 21, her brothers arranged for her to go to a college dance with one of their friends.] I said, "I don't know why we're even discussing it. I won't be allowed to go anyway." My oldest brother said, "Let me handle it."

I remember that when we got home, my brother said, "You go to your room and I'll talk to Dad." I heard loud voices in the living room and my dad saying, "No, she will not go," and my brothers saying, "Well, we're going to be there."...Finally my dad said I could go if my brother and his girlfriend drove me to the dance, and I would meet the boy at the dance, and my brother and his girlfriend would have to bring me back home. The boy was not permitted to pick me up or drive me back.... For some reason, the fellow agreed to do it that way. Of course, I never saw him again. That was my first date....

[Joanna made a career as a teacher and did not marry until she was thirty-five. Her husband, Bob Dorio, was also an Italian American.] I always said that I wasn't going to marry an Italian, because I assumed that all Italian men were as strict as my father, jealous as my father, and possessive as my father, and I wasn't going to get involved with that. But when I met Bob, he was completely different. Actually, he doesn't have much of the Italian culture, because his parents wanted to move away from that. He really isn't as Italian as I am. He is a very easygoing, great guy and is completely different....

[Joanna and Bob had two children, Brian and Lisa.] Lisa was a senior in high school this year [1988] and she wanted to go to the after-prom party after the homecoming dance. I said, "All right." I was a total wreck. I did not get any sleep. She came home at six o'clock in the morning and all I kept thinking was, "What would my father think?" I allowed this child to stay out all night! He would be just horrified!

Eleanor Cutri Smeal

In 1977, Eleanor Cutri Smeal was elected president of the National Organization for Women (NOW). As an Italian American who had experienced discrimination, she dedicated her life to combatting women's unequal role in society.

Eleanor Cutri was born in Ashtabula, Ohio, in 1939. Her father, Peter, had almost perished in an earthquake in Calabria, Italy. This near-disaster was the last straw for his family, who left for the United States in 1909. Eleanor's American-born mother, Josephine, was part of a family that had emigrated from Naples.

Eleanor's determination stems from her childhood. Her mother often told her, "You only live one life. Why should you be cheated?" However, whenever the Cutri family moved into a neighborhood, some families would shun them. "My God," Smeal recalled one of them saying, "Italians with a large family. They have four kids."

Eleanor met her husband, Charles Smeal, an engineer, while both were attending the University of Florida. After the couple, now with two children, moved to Pittsburgh, Eleanor Smeal saw the need for a women's rights movement. A painful back ailment confined her to bed and she learned that there was no disability insurance for wives and mothers.

Smeal joined the National Organization for Women in 1970 and soon was playing an active role in the organization. In 1972, she became president of the Pennsylvania branch of NOW, where she worked for equal opportunity for girls in school athletic programs.

After being elected the national president of NOW, Smeal tried to attract more housewives and mothers as members. Her efforts brought results. Within two years, the membership of NOW doubled to 100,000.

In her three terms as president, Smeal made NOW a political force to be reckoned with. Although it failed to gain passage of an Equal Rights Amendment to the Constitution, NOW successfully backed other legislation that addressed women's inequalities.

Today, Eleanor Cutri Smeal heads the Feminist Majority Fund and Foundation, an organization she helped to found in 1987. It sponsors education and research projects to empower women to take their proper role in society.

The Godfather

In early 1969, Mario Puzo's novel *The Godfather* appeared in bookstores. It was a publishing sensation, selling 1 million hardcover books and 8 million paperbacks.

Two years later, the novel was made into a movie that won even greater success. Directed by Francis Ford Coppola, who coauthored the script with Puzo, *The Godfather* won three Academy Awards, including the one for best picture. Coppola went on to make two more movies in the *Godfather* saga.

Though the creators of the book and movies were Italian Americans—as were two of the actors, Al Pacino and Robert de Niro—many Italian Americans resented the image they presented. Don Vito Corleone and his son, heroes of the story, are the heads of a closely knit crime "family." Though the word *Mafia* is not even mentioned in the films, many thought their success encouraged the stereotype of a sinister Italian American organization.

The Godfather has become part of American folklore. The phrase "Make him an offer he can't refuse" (Vito Corleone's signal to make a deadly threat) has been jokingly repeated countless times. It has even been said that the real-life criminal John Gotti adopted phrases from *The Godfather* to enhance his prestige.

Mario Puzo, the originator of the saga, grew up in a tough New York Italian American neighborhood. In his novel, a similar background gave Vito Corleone his start in crime. Puzo, of course, did not become a criminal. He developed the ambition to become a writer. After serving in the U.S. Army during World War II, he pursued his goal. His first two books were critical successes but didn't make much money. One of them, *The Fortunate Pilgrim,* is a loving portrayal of his own mother, who had to raise seven children after her husband deserted the family. Readers of *The Godfather* claim that some of its characters are also based on real-life figures. True or not, the novel brought Puzo fortune and lasting fame.

Francis Ford Coppola defended the movie by saying, "It could just as well be about the Kennedys, or the Rothschilds, about a dynasty which demands personal allegiance to the family." That may be the source of *The Godfather*'s attraction: it is the story of an immigrant family that triumphed over its enemies and attained the American dream of wealth. The Corleones might have succeeded in any other business. But many Italian Americans wish it had not been crime.

FIGHTING THE MAFIA STEREOTYPE

A woman identified only as Italia told interviewers Connie A. Maglione and Carmen Anthony Fiore why she resented the Mafia stereotype that still plagues Italian Americans.

Unfortunately, Mafia madness has obliterated every other phase of Italian contributions to American society. An Italian surname has become synonomous with crime, thanks to the constant barrage of anti-Italian themes seen regularly on TV shows such as Wiseguy, Crime Story and many others too numerous to mention. Regrettably, all Italian-Americans will suffer from this unfair stigma, in my opinion.

I hold three college degrees...putting myself through college without the benefit of government aid or minority scholarships. And I resent the depiction of Italian-Americans in the media as stupid, uneducated and tough-talking....

I cannot understand why Italian-American people accept these hideous and destructive stereotypes without complaint. No other ethnic or racial groups such as Jewish people or Black people accept these negative depictions in the media, and they are very careful and vigilant that this does not happen to them. I am fearful that Italian-Americans are becoming the last victims of vicious prejudice in this country.

Another woman, called Toni, told the interviewers how her Italian American father resisted extortion attempts by a criminal gang.

My father was extremely patriotic. He came here when he was young and never went back to Italy, never had any desire to go back. He felt that this country gave him his livelihood and he was 100 percent American, even though he loved his Italian heritage. He was patriotic to the nth degree. During the early thirties (I hate to use the word Mafia), when they were trying to get the shopkeepers to make kickbacks to get protection, he was approached by these hoodlums; he absolutely refused and told them he would turn them in to the authorities, if they made further advances. A lot of people knuckled under. He didn't. He did have the courage of his convictions. One day, when I didn't come home from school—we were off eating cherries up in a cherry tree—my mother told my father and he thought that I had been kidnapped, so he called the police. Then they found out that I was right around the corner and that I was all right. But I think there was one of those death wreaths laid on our porch at home to scare us. As far as philosophy goes, I took on a lot of my father's traits that I admired. He was a man of integrity, a man of convictions, which I have tried to pass on to my children. He was honest to a fault. He never owed a cent to anyone. Always held his head up high. He valued a good reputation.

As a United States attorney in Brooklyn, New York, Rudolph Giuliani—who became mayor of New York City in 1994—successfully prosecuted a number of organized crime leaders. Giuliani, whose grandparents arrived from Italy in the 1880s, explained his feelings about the Mafia.

In the movie The Godfather, *Marlon Brando (right), as Don Vito Corleone, turns over the leadership of the family business to his youngest son, Michael, played by Al Pacino. The scene is a sad one, for Don Corleone says he had dreamed of Michael becoming "Governor Corleone...Senator Corleone..." He waves his hand, leaving unspoken the words, "President Corleone."*

My attitude toward the Mafia stems not only from my father, who hated it, but from my grandmother, my mother's mother, who had experiences with organized crime, then known as the Black Hand, or *La Mano Nera*, that go back to the turn of the century.... She would tell me stories about the way the Black Hand and the *Camorra*, another crime gang [from Naples], acted....

My father's attitude about the Mafia probably had to do with his growing up. He saw them essentially as bullies—in other words, as people who had to band together in groups in order to have the courage to do things, rather than stand on their own. He would say to me that when he was a child growing up in New York, some of the kids that went on into the Mafia or crime gangs were really the cowards, the ones who needed three or four others to help battle their way out of situations. Banding together into gangs was a sign of being a coward rather than of a real man, who could handle himself on his own.

According to my father, the Mafia hurt Italians deeply. How? First of all, when they were an immigrant community, by being bullies, banding together, and threatening to break up their stores. By preying on them, taking what little money they could accumulate, acting as parasites. In a more general way, they hurt Italians and gave them a bad name by creating stereotypes that other people used to poke fun at....

The fact that I [as a prosecutor of Mafia figures] have an Italian name, I hope, will help to dispel, to some extent at least, the unfair prejudice and the unfair stereotype. When I first got into this area of [prosecuting] crime and became more aware of how the Italian-American community feels about this, how hurt they are by it, I thought that there would be some value to my being an Italian-American, because as people read revelations about what the Mafia has done, they will see a couple of Italian names involved in investigating and prosecuting. This will present a different image of Italian-Americans to them and will tell the community and the world that they can do a pretty effective job of cleaning up these problems.

Matteo Accetta, a recent immigrant from Trappeto, Sicily, lives in San Pedro, near Los Angeles, California. One of the medallions around his neck is shaped like the island of Sicily.

Italian immigrants started to move into the North End of Boston in the 1880s. Today, the neighborhood remains home to many Italian American families who proudly celebrate their heritage and traditions.

MAKING IT

In the drive for success, many Italian Americans experience conflicts about losing the family values that propelled them in the first place. As Joseph Giordano wrote in 1980:

My grandfather was born in Naples and came to this country in the late 1800s. He worked as an unskilled laborer and lived in poverty most of his life.

My father, the oldest of my grandfather's eight children, was a journeyman steamfitter and, together with my mother, raised three sons and a daughter. I, the youngest, was the first to go to college and become a professional.

In only three generations, the Giordanos, like millions of other Italian-American families, have moved from poverty to working class to middle class—from the ethnic neighborhood to suburbia.

Italian Americans can be said to have "made it." But what, precisely, do we mean when we say we have "arrived"?

According to the National Opinion Research Center in Chicago, Italian Americans of the second and third generations have significantly closed the income "gap," and are catching up with some of the more prosperous ethnic groups. We are now the third most economically successful religio-ethnic group in America, behind Jews and Irish Catholics. This development is particularly significant because the Italians who immigrated to the United States were among the most illiterate of the ethnic groups....

But "making it" by American society's economic and social standards is only half the story. For the Italian American, the issue of success is especially complex, involving feelings and attitudes about personal identity and familial relationships.

It's often hard to negotiate a comfortable balance between the traditional values of the family and the demands for achievement in the larger society. The message we get from outside the family is to "be an individual," to "achieve," to "make it"—even if it is necessary to break away from the family, neighborhood, and the culture of your grandparents in the process.

In the home, particularly in second- and third-generation families, we often get conflicting messages. In my family, my father would overtly encourage me—"Get ahead, make something of yourself." But then there were the unspoken words that were in many ways more powerful. "Don't change. Stay close to home."…

While Papa was proud that I graduated from college and that I had entered graduate school, he was not too sure what I was doing in school.

He once boasted to the men on his job about the fact that I was getting my masters degree in social work. They were unimpressed; social work was not high on their list of status jobs. At home that night, he expressed his disappointment in my choice of profession by asking, "Why do you want to give handouts to people on the corner?"

Papa died before realizing that my path, while different from the one he envisioned, did achieve the recognition he so desired for me—and himself. I wish he were here to share in it....

Maintaining close ties to the family and at the same time wanting to "get ahead" will continue to be a dilemma for second, third, and fourth generations. "Should I take the promotion and move to another city away from our families and friends?" "If I work overtime, I'll make more money or get a better position—but then I am away from the kids." "I want to go to college, or get a job, but my mother tells me I should stay home with the babies—and my husband agrees with my mother."

There are no easy solutions. I believe that, for Italians, the family is the secret of our survival. It has lasted for thousands of years, surviving poverty, famine, wars, governments, and immigration to foreign lands. It is here to stay.

But, to keep the family strong we need to recognize and deal with powerful forces of change in our society. We can continue to be nourished by the support of the family and, at the same time, go out into the larger society to pursue our goals. The challenge will be to see that the current generation and those to follow will receive the benefits of both worlds.

Tony Bennett (born Benedetto) is one of the best of the romantic singers in the Sinatra tradition. He grew up in Queens, New York, and attributes part of his singing success to his Italian heritage.

My singing abilities come from my father. He had a beautiful singing voice. We were very oriented to music. The whole family—my mother, father, aunts, uncles—got together on the weekends and sang and played music. It was during the Depression and the big entertainment was gathering the children and having them entertain the grown-ups. My brother and I sang, and together with my sister, we put on shows with singing and acting for the aunts and uncles. I remember them very well. I don't have total recall, but I remember the good vibrations, the warm feeling that we got from one another, and the fun we had.

My brother was a tremendous singer in those days. His name was Giovanni Benedetto, and he was called the little Caruso. He sang at the Metropolitan Opera and did solo spots; he also went on radio. He became the hero of the family. When he came out of the service at the end of World War II, he did not continue in music. He had a large family of children and

Joe DiMaggio

On October 1, 1949, baseball fans celebrated Joe DiMaggio Day at Yankee Stadium. As 70,000 spectators watched, Di Maggio said, "I want to thank the good Lord for making me a Yankee." But the Yankee Clipper had fans far beyond New York. DiMaggio had the special charisma of a superstar and was regarded as the greatest baseball player of his time.

Joseph Paul DiMaggio, Jr., was born in Martinez, California, on November 25, 1914. His parents had emigrated from an island off Sicily. Young Joe grew up in San Francisco's Little Italy on Russian Hill. Playing baseball for a boys club team, he was the only boy without a uniform, an expense his family could not afford. Before long, however, he was playing for the San Francisco Seals, a minor league club.

Scouts for the New York Yankees saw his talent and signed him up. From his first season, the 21-year-old outfielder was a star. He was chosen for the All-Star game, as he would be every year of his career. With his first earnings, he bought a home for his parents.

DiMaggio took off as a national sports hero in 1941. It started with a hit on May 15th. Game after game, he came through with another hit. Reporters began to wonder if he would reach the previous record of 44 games. Radio announcers broke into programs to report his mounting streak. When someone stole his lucky bat, radio stations broadcast an appeal to the thief to return it–and he did. DiMaggio broke the record on July 2 and went on to hit safely in 11 more games. His 56-game streak is a record that still holds.

During World War II, DiMaggio exchanged his $43,000 baseball salary for the $50 monthly pay of a private in the U.S Army. In 1946, he returned to the Yankees. When he retired in 1951, he had a lifetime batting average of .325. In the years since, DiMaggio has remained a popular figure, though he shuns publicity.

Frank Sinatra

"The kid's name is Sinatra," the band leader Harry James said to a reporter in 1939. "He considers himself the greatest vocalist in the business. Get that! Not even one hit record. No one ever heard of him. He looks like a wet rag. But he says he is the greatest." The 24-year-old "kid," however, would make good on his claim to greatness. Over a career of more than 50 years, Frank Sinatra has won millions of fans all over the world.

Francis Albert Sinatra was born in Hoboken, New Jersey, on December 12, 1915. He was the only child of Anthony and Natalie Sinatra, both born in Italy. In his teens, Sinatra and three friends formed a group called the Hoboken Four, which won first prize on the "Amateur Hour" radio program. Harry James heard Sinatra on a local radio station and signed him to a contract.

Sinatra soon shifted to Tommy Dorsey's band, which toured the country. During this time, Sinatra developed his distinctive style of singing. He sought to imitate the flowing quality of Dorsey's trombone with his voice, swimming laps to increase his breath control. His first hit recording, "I'll Never Smile Again," made him a national star.

Then at the end of the 1940s, his voice started to give out. It looked as if his singing career were finished. Hearing that the novel *From Here to Eternity* was to be made into a movie, Sinatra took a screen test for the role of Private Maggio. It brought him the Academy Award for best supporting actor in 1953.

With his movie career established, his singing voice returned. Now it had a deeper and richer tone. The albums of American pop classics he recorded during the 1950s are still regarded as among the finest ever made.

When rock and roll began to dominate American popular music, Sinatra refused to shift to a rock style. His career never flagged. "My Way," an anthem for his attitude toward life, became a favorite with audiences in concert halls and nightclubs. In live performance, on screen, and in the recording studio, Sinatra, dubbed the Chairman of the Board, has remained one of the most popular American entertainers. In 1993, nearing his 80th birthday, he recorded yet another hit album, "Duets," collaborating with many current pop stars.

had to find steady work to support them. He lives in Florida now. He is very happy.

My dad was born in Calabria, which is at the southern tip of Italy. He was a very intelligent guy. He came over here, an immigrant, and chose Fifty-second Street and Sixth Avenue in Manhattan, right down the street from where I live now, as his first grocery store. It was right in the heart of town. He picked the right address. That was about 1922 or '23. I was born in 1926. But then he took ill and the doctor said that he should get away from city life. So we moved to Astoria, in the borough of Queens, which was really country in those days. There were sheep and goats where people walk now; it was farm country. Imagine! But he was a sickly man and died when I was nine years old.

Many guys say this about their mothers, but my mother was really quite exceptional. She was a fantastic lady who raised my brother, sister, and myself all by herself after my father died. My older sister helped; she took over a motherly role. My mom was born in Little Italy in Manhattan, on Mott and Hester Streets. After my father died, she worked in the garment center as a seamstress and then came home to look after the house and kids....

I learned many things from her without her teaching me. As a seamstress, she never worked on a cheap or badly conceived dress. The only time I ever saw her get angry was the day she had a bad dress to work on. Later on, I found myself subconsciously turning down all bad songs and realizing only until much later that I learned about refusing the second-rate from her. If I am going to do a song, I want to sing the very best song and not compromise. That is what she taught us: Work with the best. Not to compromise is a marvelous thing to learn. In our kind of materialistic society, our only concern is making money, but you know, you have to keep your integrity to have some peace within yourself. Just to make money is not enough; that is greedy. Keeping your integrity, you *can* produce and make money. It gives you a quiet dignity and substance. Otherwise, you feel unhappy.

Italian Americans were caught up with pazzia Americana *(American craziness)—their term for the enthusiasm Americans have for sports. The pazzia included all sports, but baseball was the first in which Italian Americans excelled. Yogi Berra, a Hall of Fame player for the New York Yankees, recalls:*

My parents were born in a town north of Milan called Malvoglia, near the Swiss border. My dad came over to America first, and my mom stayed in Italy until he got established. My two older brothers were born in Italy. I was born in St. Louis....

We lived on what we called the Hill in St. Louis. They were all Italian on the Hill, so all my friends had to be Italian. We all got along fine. Everybody knew each other and we had good neighbors. You still have a lot of Italians left on the Hill. It hasn't thinned out.

My parents spoke a dialect in the house, a Milanese dialect—at least, that is what mom and dad called it. I think now, in Italy, it is all one language, Italian, that everyone speaks and the dialects aren't being spoken so much. Before, each town had a different dialect. We had a lot of Italians from all over Italy on the Hill, and I didn't know what they were saying. I couldn't understand them. Some words I knew, but not the way I could understand my mom and dad. We tried to get them to speak American, too. They spoke broken English. But most of the time my brothers and sister spoke Italian to them.

There were four brothers in the family, and my sister came last. We felt all right about her. She was a little spoiled....

As a kid, I just wanted to play ball.

My father didn't know what baseball was. He wasn't anxious for me to play ball. My older brothers were all ballplayers, too. He didn't believe in sports. They had to go to work. But they said to him, 'Let *him* go (meaning me, the youngest boy) We're all working.' And he let me....

I *always* liked to play ball. I didn't need to be inspired by other Italian Americans, like Joe DiMaggio. Anyway, I was a St. Louis fan. Joe, a Yankee, was never my favorite.

Al Santoli, Sr., came to the United States as an infant in 1921. His father had arrived a year earlier, and with his earnings as a construction laborer bought a home for his family in the Corlett area of Cleveland, Ohio. Al's father encouraged him to get an education, and eventually he worked for NASA, the National Aeronautics and Space Administration. In 1988, Al reminisced about his life to his son, Al Santoli, Jr., a noted Italian American writer.

World War II changed a lot of things for my generation of immigrants. Not the old folks so much, but the young. We came home from the military with much higher confidence and expectations. We all bought cars and branched out away from our ethnic boundaries....

I broke with the old Italian tradition of living close to my parents and moved to another area of Cleveland, which was closer to where I worked....

My first child was born in June 1949. And in 1950, just before the air base [where he worked] was closed, my second child, Gloria, was born. Because of the kids, my wife and I decided to move to a larger home back in my old neighborhood....

For the next thirty years, I worked as a representative of the Defense Supply Agency in private industry. I attended eighteen different colleges and schools and earned the equivalent of degrees in chemical and mechanical engineering, and in industrial management...

Even though I was moving up in education and job responsibility, my wife and I and our three children—Albert, Gloria, and Donna—stayed in the old neighborhood until 1961. By that time, just about everyone I grew up with had moved to the

Lee Iacocca

On August 15, 1983, the Chrysler Corporation climbed out of debt. Four years earlier, the company had been on the verge of bankruptcy. But Chrysler's dynamic new president, Lee Iacocca, had persuaded Congress to grant it a loan to stay afloat. Now, with Chrysler starting to make money, Lee Iacocca became a business folk hero.

Lido Anthony Iacocca was born in Allentown, Pennsylvania, on October 15, 1924. His parents were Italian immigrants from a town north of Naples. From the age of 16, Lee wanted to work in the auto business. His family had always owned Ford cars, and in 1945, he entered the company's executive training program. When he was assigned to the engineering branch, however, he quit. He felt his talents lay in sales and marketing.

Iacocca persuaded Ford's eastern district sales manager to hire him. He created a sales campaign that let customers buy new Fords with payments of only $56 a month. Its success caught the eye of the top brass at Ford. In 1960, Iacocca was named general manager of the Ford division.

Iacocca's greatest triumph at Ford was the Mustang–a moderately priced sedan that looked like a sports car. Wildly popular with young people, the Mustang became one of the best-selling cars in Detroit's history. It also propelled Iacocca to the top of the executive ladder. On December 10, 1970, Henry Ford II named Iacocca president of the company.

However, the son of immigrants did not get along well with the millionaire heir to the Ford fortune. In 1978, Henry Ford fired Iacocca.

The Chrysler Corporation offered Iacocca its presidency. Accepting the challenge, he rushed into production the K car, a fuel-efficient auto to compete with popular Japanese imports. Iacocca often appeared in the company's TV ads, urging customers to "buy American." There was even an Iacocca boom for President in 1984, before he made it clear that politics was not for him.

However, he volunteered to be chairman of the Statue of Liberty-Ellis Island Foundation. He felt a special pride in helping to plan the celebration of the statue's centennial in 1986. It was a reminder of his own immigrant roots as well as those of millions of other Americans.

Antonin Scalia

In June 1986, President Ronald Reagan nominated Antonin Scalia to the Supreme Court. For Scalia, known to his friends as Nino, it was the culmination of a brilliant career. At the age of 50, he became the first Italian American Supreme Court Justice.

Antonin Scalia was born on March 11, 1936, in an Italian neighborhood of Trenton, New Jersey. His father, Eugene Scalia, a Sicilian immigrant, became a professor at Brooklyn College. His mother, Catherine Panaro Scalia, taught elementary school.

Antonin was a brilliant student, graduating first in his class in high school and again at Georgetown University. At Harvard Law School, Scalia earned a reputation as a forceful debater and was editor of the Law Review.

After a stint at a corporate law firm and teaching at the University of Virginia Law School, Scalia received his first government post. President Richard Nixon named him general counsel for the White House office of telecommunications policy in 1971. Scalia later served in the Justice Department as well.

Leaving government in 1981, Scalia built a reputation for his conservative views as a professor at Georgetown Law Center and the University of Chicago Law School. He attacked the Supreme Court's 1973 *Roe* v. *Wade* decision, which recognized a woman's constitutional right to an abortion. He also blasted court-ordered affirmative-action programs for schools and businesses.

These conservative views brought Scalia to the attention of the Reagan administration. In 1982, he was named to the U.S. Court of Appeals, where his decisions made him the front runner to fill an opening on the Supreme Court in 1986. The clincher was his interview with President Reagan, who liked Scalia's warm personality. After receiving the highest rating from the American Bar Association, Scalia was confirmed by the Senate without one negative vote.

Since then, Justice Scalia has been a strong force in moving the Supreme Court toward more conservative positions on issues. His strong intellect, elegant writing style, and personality have given him great influence with his colleagues on the Court.

new suburbs that were being built just outside the city. Cleveland's ethnic neighborhoods were breaking up. My family was becoming part of the American melting pot....

Financially, the move was a leap of faith. I was paid a government salary, which in those days was not more than $12,000. We looked at a numbr of housing developments that were being built before we decided on South Euclid. When we moved in the street wasn't even paved....

The house cost $19,000. That doesn't seem like much today, but on my small salary, and with three growing kids, there were many months when we weren't sure if we could make our payments. What saved us was that my wife is a terrific bookkeeper. She knows how to budget and make every dollar stretch. And I never spent money on vacations. During the summer, I'd take a couple weeks off from work to paint the house and do whatever repairs were needed....

In 1963, NASA began the Apollo Program to send a spacecraft to the moon.... I was assigned to the Space Program Division at TRW [a defense contractor]....

The work was incredibly challenging both in the areas of scientific progress being made and in the speed and demands of our production schedule....

The TRW shop where I worked was in a huge manufacturing and assembly factory that was built in an old farm field. Some of the old farmhouses were still used as office buildings. The noise level from all of the giant machinery...was a constant roar. My team workers and I had to practically shout to hear each other over the sound....

When I came home from work at night, my wife and kids

always asked me why I was talking so loud at the dinner table. I couldn't help it....

Just this week, after many years away from the shop, I went to see the doctor because I've lost a lot of my hearing. It's what I call "shop ear." The doc says I probably need to wear hearing aids. I guess that was one of the occupational hazards. But, looking back at what we accomplished during those years, I have no regrets....

All of us in the program realized that we were on the cutting edge of history. Whenever a spacecraft went up successfully, we were elated. I felt a deep pride that, to this day, I have a difficult time expressing....

On July 20, 1969, it was an incredible feeling to watch the Apollo 11 space shot on television as our astronaut Neil Armstrong walked on the moon. I thought of the small farm town I came from in the mountains of Italy, where people were lucky to attend elementary school and didn't even have plumbing or running water in their homes.

The Italian American writer Tina De Rosa, who grew up in Chicago, expressed the conflict between the old ways and the American success story.

What happens to a person who is raised in a passionate, furious, comic and tragic emotional climate, where the ghost of one's grandmother is as real as the food on one's plate?... What happens to the person who is raised in this environment, and then finds herself in a world where the highest emotional charge comes with the falling of the Dow Jones average, or yet another rise in the price of gold?

Italian American weddings are still festive occasions. On the opposite page, white doves are released over the wedding party of Annalisa Vottola and Edward Ogle in San Pedro, California. Above, the bride and groom greet their friends and relatives on the steps of Maria Stella Maris (Mary, Star of the Sea) Church.

Geraldine Ferraro

When Geraldine Ferraro stood on the podium with Walter Mondale at the Democratic Convention in 1984, a milestone had been reached in American political history. She was both the first woman and the first Italian American to be nominated by a major party for Vice President of the United States. Though she lost the election, she made history.

Geraldine Ferraro was born in 1935 in Newburg, New York. After her father, an immigrant from a town north of Naples, died, Geraldine's mother, Antonetta, moved the family to Queens, a borough of New York City. Geraldine remembered that her mother wanted both her and her brother Carl to get a good education. In one area, however, they were treated differently. "Where Carl had it a little easier," Geraldine recalled, "got a little more, was...that he was allowed to go out. I wasn't allowed to date until I was seventeen."

After college, Geraldine Ferraro married John Zaccaro. While raising their three children, she found time to go to law school at night. After passing her bar exam, she served as an assistant district attorney.

Ferraro entered politics, winning a seat in the U.S. Congress. In the House of Representatives, she became known as a moderate liberal. Though she was a Catholic, she dissented from the Catholic church's position by endorsing a woman's right to have an abortion.

After being nominated for Vice President in 1984, she ran a vigorous campaign. Unfortunately, she faced a flurry of rumors and innuendos about her husband's finances and links to the Mafia. Ferraro felt bitter about the campaign, and in 1992 she resumed her political career.

When she ran for the Democratic party's nomination for a U.S. Senate seat in 1992, the same kinds of rumors surfaced again, and she narrowly lost the hard-fought campaign.

However, Ferraro has remained in the public eye because of her historic role. She is proud that her three children all are studying Italian and can speak it better than she can. She has not ruled out another run for office but will always be remembered as a trailblazer for women and for Italian Americans.

PIZZA, PASTA, AND MORE

Food has always played a central role in the Italian home. Theresa F. Bucchieri recalls her grandmother's cooking in her Sicilian family's home in South Philadelphia. On the ground floor, the Bucchieri family ran their own grocery store.

The kitchen, although square and spacious, was the coziest spot in our nine-room house in South Philadelphia, and our grocery store the most fascinating spot. The kitchen was always fragrant with delicious smells, and the store was the charming (and intriguing) old fashioned type of Italian grocery, stocked with an appetizing variety of salami, cheese, sauces, relishes, spices and pastas of all shapes and sizes.....

While Mom and Pop tended the store, Nonna Serafina (Mom's mother) reigned over the kitchen. She was strong, of average height, and a dynamo of energy. She had an olive complexion with laughing brown eyes and snowy white hair. A look of joy always suffused her face and this was unquestionably generated straight from her heart....She was always partial to gray, brown, green, and lilac paisley and polka dot dresses which she loved to wear with colorful starched aprons....

I fondly recall climbing on a chair to watch Nonna "stir up" magic in the family kitchen. Later on I was her adoring apprentice!

Then in the store I used to love to weigh the pasta—no packaged macaroni in those days...and Pop used to put the pasta in the counter bins with glass windows so that the customers could see the shape and size of the macaroni. But, best of all, I used to love to cut the salami! That was before the electric meat cutters. I developed a knack for cutting the salami thin so that a quarter-pound looked like a lot. Because of this skill, many a time Mom would call to me, "Teresina, please come out in the store and cut some salami for Donna [Mrs.] Filomena." The delicatessen meat counter was by the window in complete view of passersby, and many times when I would look up from the counter I would see my young friends of the neighborhood outside with their noses pressed against the window pane, watching me, perhaps with a little envy, as I "went to town" cutting the salami.

Nonna hailed from Serro, which is in Messina, Sicily, where both my parents were born, the Sicily glorified by legend and history. Nonna always sang the praises of her *Bedda Sicilia*. She used to enchant us children (my brother, Johnny, two years my junior, and my sister, Sara, eight years my junior), with Sicilian folklore and Sicilian history. She never let us forget the fact that Sicily was the crossroads of the Mediterra-

"St. Joseph's Table," an elaborate display of food on the saint's feast day, March 19, is an Italian American tradition. It is said to have begun centuries ago on Sicily, when people prayed to the island's patron saint to end a famine. When the rains fell and the crops were harvested, the peasants filled Saint Joseph's shrines with a feast of thanksgiving. This one was prepared in Pueblo, Colorado, in 1990.

nean and, because of its strategic position, many people ruled the island. Among them were Phoenicians, Greeks, Romans, Cathaginians, Saracens, Normans, Germans, and the French and the Spanish, all of whom left imperishable traces of their cultures and civilizations. And, she would conclude triumphantly, they left their mark on the kitchen, too!...

Good food, Nonna would remind us, brings contentment and love. Through the medium of the mixing bowl I got to know and cherish my wonderful Nonna. Every dish or meal that she prepared became a culinary adventure as far as she and all of us were concerned because it invariably was associated with some festive occasion, legend, custom, or bit of folklore. During our life with Nonna, our table was lovingly laden with food, presented with the traditions and rituals that accompanied it. We children have treasured them and have tried to give them life in our own respective households.

Nonna Serafina went to her eternal reward at the tender age of 94. Even now, I chuckle when I enjoy a dish that has a familiar taste. I can almost see Nonna hustling and bustling in Heaven treating the saints, whom she feted on earth during the Feast days, to some of her culinary masterpieces!

Today, preparing a festive meal at home or smelling the aroma of good cooking anywhere brings me ever so near to Nonna, and, no matter where I am traveling, whenever I see a corner, old-fashioned Italian grocery store with cheese and salamis dangling in the window, an indescribable feeling surges in my heart and I feel so close to my wonderful Mom and Pop.

For years, Mamma Leone's Italian restaurant was a New York landmark. Her son, Gene, describes how it came about:

Mother Leone's restaurant was born on Mother's thirty-second birthday.... Enrico Caruso, the great tenor and a close friend of the family, was among the guests at Mother's birthday party. He was the man most responsible for getting Mother to open her little Italian restaurant. "*Un piccolo posticino,*" as he called it.

Mother first heard of her party on the morning of her birthday, November 2, 1905. As Father was leaving the house he turned and said, "Oh, by the way, Luisa, for your birthday I've invited a few of our friends from the Metropolitan Opera House back here for dinner tonight after their rehearsal."

"Good," Mother said, "*Quanti saranno?*" (How many will there be?)

"Oh, there'll be a few," he answered. "*Una cinquantina.*" (About fifty.)

This news might have floored the average housewife, but not Mother. She just smiled and said, "Fine, I'll get busy right away. I'll prepare a magnificent dinner for you."

The fact that she would be tied up all day in the kitchen didn't bother her a bit. There is nothing in this world that Mother enjoyed more than making her friends happy with her fabulous cooking.

A CHRISTMAS DELIGHT

Theresa Bucchieri remembered her childhood Christmas:

One of the things I have never forgotten was Christmas morning at our house. We children would hear Nonna [grandmother] hustling and bustling toward our bedroom. We would pretend to be asleep, but she would bend over us, smothering us with bear hugs and kisses. She would greet us with "*Buon giorno, tesoro*" [Good morning, my treasures], and she would beckon us with "Come and see what Santa Claus brought you."…

We would scamper down the stairs to the living room and before we all sat down to breakfast we opened our gifts and "oohed" and "aahed" with joy.…

The featured item of the Christmas breakfast was a delicious wine custard called zabaglione. Many have this custard for dessert but we used to enjoy it and still do at breakfast, especially on Christmas and Easter Sunday. Here is the recipe.

ZABAGLIONE

In top of double boiler, beat nine egg yolks, gradually adding 4 1/2 tbs. sugar and 6 tbs. Marsala wine (which is like sherry). Cook over hot but not boiling water, beating constantly with egg beater until very thick. Serve hot and 6 people will be delighted!

Pasta is one of the great gifts of Italian Americans to the United States. Originally taken to Italy from China by Marco Polo, the basic mix of flour, water, and eggs was molded and strung into countless shapes. The most popular form is still the long strands known as spaghetti, *or "little cords."*

Italians were the first to combine pasta with cheese, producing such delicious mixtures as ravioli *("little turnips") and* tortellini *("little cakes"). Canned or dried varieties, available in every supermarket, are not nearly as delicious as the fresh kind that this restaurant chef is preparing.*

She took my older brother Joe and me to Paddy's Market on the West Side to buy all the necessary foods. We borrowed the meatman's pushcart and returned with a load of fine foods.

Soon, Mother was cooking and singing away to her heart's content. It wasn't long before she had her sauces simmering and the cacciatora on the fire. The whole stuffed chickens, sprinkled with rosemary and covered with slices of salted pork and with some olive oil poured over them, were roasting slowly in the oven.

The kitchen and the wine cellar, where the party was going to be held, were filled with the grand fragrance and aroma of Mother's mouth-watering cooking. She was busy but happy.

She set to work preparing the many varieties of antipasto that only she could dream up. She made the sauce for her shrimps that was so delicious that I couldn't stop until I dunked more than half a loaf of bread into it.

Sixty guests showed up....

A long table, the full length of the wine cellar, was loaded with many of Mother's antipasto dishes, ravioli, bowls of cacciatora, trays of whole roast chicken, platters of bugie [fried dessert pastries], loaves of good-crusted Italian bread, Parmesan and Swiss cheeses and lots of luscious fresh fruits. My brother Joe and I were kept hopping, helping Mother take care of the guests. Joe was nine years old and I was seven....

Papa filled the wineglasses, and this was what everyone was waiting for. They knew that as soon as the maestro began playing, the room would be filled with music and singing. Sure enough, as soon as he went into an aria, the first to sing was the great Caruso.

As Caruso lifted his glorious voice in song, so did the thirty members of the Met's singing chorus. He sang an aria from *Lucia di Lammermoor* and his clear notes made the glasses on the table tinkle. The chorus, a fine collection of beautiful voices, had such power that the walls seemed to vibrate and I thought sure the streets were trembling. Any one of the chorus singers might have been a star in his own right had he had the opportunity and the funds to study under the great voice teachers of the time. Listening to the music was like having a private opera, sung by the world's greatest company, right in our own home.

This, to Father, was living. He was never happier than when he was surrounded by his friends, music, singing, Mother's delicious food and his own good wine. Papa, believing that he could sing, especially when the party was in his own cellar, often sang duets with Caruso. The way I remember it, half of the duet sounded wonderful.

The glorious singing continued and there was plenty of good food and good wine being consumed, too. Caruso, seated with Arturo Vigna, Giacomo Puccini, Pasquale Amato, Antonio Scotti, Giulio Gatti-Casazza and Nellie Melba, was enjoying a dish of Mother's ravioli. Delight was written all over his face.

"Luisa," he said in his booming voice, "like fine wine you improve with age. Tonight you have outdone yourself with this magnificent feast. I am convinced that you are the greatest cook in the world."

Then for about the hundredth time, he asked when she was going to open that *piccolo posticino, solamenta per noi* (little restaurant, just for us).

Looking around, Mother visualized this as her own little restaurant. The wine was flowing, the food was delicious, the piano was playing, Puccini and Arturo Vigna were conducting the Anvil Chorus from *Il Trovatore*, and no one in the room seemed to have a care in the world.

This had to be a great moment in anyone's life, and Mother, who had a marvelous sense of timing, knew this was the chance to get what she wanted. To open a restaurant had been her dream for a long, long time. But Father, like most Italian husbands, didn't like the idea of his wife working. Whenever she spoke of opening a restaurant, which she did frequently, he said no. And papa was *il padrone* (the boss)....

But Mother now was really convinced and more determined than ever that...this night, her birthday, might be the right time to have her dream come true.

She turned to Caruso. "Enrico," she asked, "do you really believe that I could run a good restaurant?"

"Certainly," he practically shouted, "with food like this?"

"Well then," she added, "let's ask Gerome right now."

Caruso took Mother by the hand and went over to Papa, who was singing the quartet from *Rigoletto* with Amato, Scotti and Melba. Father was singing the tenor's part and Caruso joined in "to help out."

When the serenade ended, Caruso threw his arm around Papa's shoulder, gave him a little squeeze and said, "Gerolamo, will you allow Lusia to open our little restaurant?"

Papa looked straight into Mama's eyes and asked, "Luisa, are you serious? Do you really want a restaurant?"

Mother never blinked an eye.

"Yes," she said, "do you think I've been joking all these years? There is nothing I want more."

Father hesitated and then continued, "Do you know what it means, how hard you'll have to work?"

Mother laughed. "Who's afraid of hard work? I love it!"

So Papa gave his permission and Mother went on to follow his good advice. He told her, "Luisa, I will not have anything to do with your restaurant, but please remember, decorate the plate, not the place."

Mamma Leone's restaurant opened on April 27, 1906, and the first customer was Enrico Caruso. It remained a favorite Manhattan dining place until 1994.

Some claim that pizza is the most popular American food. It offers bread, vegetable, and dairy products all in a single bite. But Italian American pizza lovers will tell you that it tastes best when baked in a forno, *a wood-fired oven like this one made by Andy Briguglio in his backyard.*

FESTA!

Among the pleasures of life in the Italian American communities were the festas celebrated in honor of popular saints. Richard Gambino, a first-generation American, remembered the San Gennaro festival of his childhood.

At the two-week-long festival of San Gennaro, held annually in New York's Little Italy, donations are made at a picture of the saint.

Their aromas of food, the sight of burly men swaying from side to side and lurching forward under the weight of enormous statues of exotic Madonnas and saints laden with money and gifts, the music of the Italian bands in uniforms with dark-peaked caps, white shirts, and black ties and the bright arches of colored lights spanning the city streets are essential memories of my childhood, as they are of many second-generation Italian Americans. True to the spirit of *campanalismo*, each group of *paesani* in New York had its own *festa*. People from Catania celebrated Sant' Agata, who according to legend saved the ancient city from destruction by lava during one of Mount Etna's more violent outbursts. The people from Palermo honored their saint, Santa Rosalia, who saved Palermo from pestilence.

Robert Orsi described in detail the annual festa of the Madonna of 115th Street in Manhattan. Similar festas were—and still are—held in Italian American neighborhoods, honoring their own patron saints.

Shortly after midnight on July 16, the great bell high in the campanile of the church of Our Lady of Mount Carmel on 115th Street announced to East Harlem that the day of the festa had begun. It was a solemn moment; the voice of the bell seemed more vibrant and sonorous on this night. The sound touched every home in Italian Harlem. It greeted the devout already arriving from the other boroughs and from Italian communities in Connecticut, New Jersey, Pennsylvania, and even California....

The Italians of East Harlem had been preparing for the festa for weeks.... The homes...had been scrubbed clean, the windows had been washed and the floor polished. Residents had bought and cooked special foods in anticipation of the arrival of their guests....

The time of the festa was long and undefined. Some people say it lasted two or three days, others say a week, even two weeks. It was a celebration that knew no time.... Italian Harlem slept little during the days of the festa. Children played with their cousins from New Haven and Boston and then fell asleep in the laps of the adults, who stayed up all night talking and eating. People went out into the crowded streets at two or three in the morning to go to confession or attend a special mass at the church that had been offered to *la Madonna* for the health of their mother or in the hope of finding a job. When they returned, there was more eating and talking and visiting.

Then sometime in the early afternoon of July 16, people would begin walking over to the church. They were dressed in their finest clothes, particularly the children, whose new outfits their families had bought at considerable sacrifice but also with the fierce determination that the family should make *bella figura* [a good appearance] in the community and show proper *rispetto* [respect] for the Virgin on her feast day....

Vendors of religious articles set up booths along the sidewalks, competing for business with the thriving local trade in religious goods. The booths were filled with wax replicas of internal human organs and with models of human limbs and heads. Someone who had been healed—or hoped to be healed—by the Madonna of headaches or arthritis would carry wax models of the afflicted limbs or head, painted to make them look realistic, in the big procession. The devout could also buy little wax statues of infants. Charms to ward off the evil eye, such as little horns to wear around the neck and little red hunchbacks, were sold alongside the holy cards, statues of Jesus, Mary, and the saints, and the wax body parts.

The most sought-after items were the big and enormously heavy candles that the faithful bought, carried all through the blistering July procession, and then donated to the church.... The weights of the candles chosen by the people corresponded to the seriousness of the grace they were asking....A bad problem or a great hope required an especially heavy candle....In 1923, for example, Giuseppe Caparo, sixty-nine years old, who had recently fallen from the fifth floor of a building without hurting himself, offered the Madonna a candle weighing as much as he did, 185 pounds. If, as often happened, the candles were too long or too heavy to be carried by one person, other family members and friends would share the burden.

The most characteristic sensuous facts of the Mount Carmel festa were the smell and taste of food.... Big meals,

Rosaries made in Italy are sold at the festival of Our Lady of Mt. Carmel in Hammonton, New Jersey.

At every Italian American festival, an abundance of food is available. Among the favorites are calzone *(a pastry roll with pizza-type fillings) and* zeppole *(a pastry roll filled with fruit, chocolate, or other sweets).*

As Others Saw Them

Columbus Day has always had a special meaning for Italian immigrants, who take pride in the fact that the sailor born in Genoa was the first European to reach the New World. The newspaper in the little town of Herrin, Illinois, recorded one gala celebration in 1905:

Guido Spagnolina, a veteran balloon maker from Italy, is preparing to build one of the largest and most gorgeously illuminated paper balloons ever sent up in this country. He is planning one 25 feet high and decorated with 500 candles. As the balloon ascends and gets up four or five hundred feet, the candles that festoon it become detached and drop to the earth like shooting meteors....His large balloon made for Columbus Day will be a duplicate of the one with which he won the first prize at the Florence festival.... Louis Oldani was instructed to go to St. Louis and purchase regalia...that will be used for the parade. It will be a brilliant historical pageant. The streets of Herrin will resemble a festival day of the 16th century. There will be men in armor, mounted horsemen, courtiers, cavaliers, 15th-century sailors, floats resembling the old sailing vessels in which Columbus and his men crossed the Atlantic.

A Columbus Day parade in Walla Walla, Washington, in the early 1910s. Italian Americans take great pride in the fact that the first European visitor to the New World was an Italian.

pranzi, were cooked in the homes, and after the festa, family, friends, and neighbors would gather for long and boisterous meals. During the day, snacks of hard-boiled eggs, sausage, and pastry were ready at home. But it was in the street that the real eating took place. From the street vendors the devout could buy beans boiled in oil and red pepper, hot waffles, fried and sugared dough, boiled corn, ice cream, watermelon, sausage, "tempting pies filled with tomato, red pepper and garlic," bowls of pasta, dried nuts, nougat candy, raisins, tinted cakes, and "pastry rings glistening in the light."...

The crowds slowly made their way to the Church of Our Lady of Mount Carmel....The front of the church was decorated with colored lights that traced the outline of the facade and spelled out "Nostra Signora del Monte Carmelo." It was on the steps of the church that the intensity and diversity of the day were at their extreme. Penitents crawled up the steps on their hands and knees, some of them dragging their tongues along the stone. Thousands of people were jammed onto 115th Street in front of the church in the crushing July heat and humidity. Nuns and volunteers from the parish moved through the crowd to help those who succumbed.... The crowd had been gathering since midnight, and as the time of the procession neared...the excitement sizzled like the heat....

In the afternoon, after the solemn high mass, parish and neighborhood societies began to take their places in front of the church in preparation for the procession...Behind the societies, a large statue of the Madonna...was mounted on a float which had been decorated with flowers and white ribbons. An honor guard of little girls and young unmarried women clothed in white surrounded the Madonna. Dressed in their best suits...the young men from the Holy Name Society who would be pulling the float through the streets of East Harlem—a task that was viewed as a great honor and privilege—lined up in front of the Madonna. When everyone was in place, the banner of the Congregazione del Monte Carmelo was carried out by male members of the congregation. Then, at a signal from the priests and with an explosion of music and fireworks, the procession began....

As la Madonna slowly made her way through the streets of East Harlem, the devout standing on the sidewalks in front of their tenements kicked off their shoes and joined the procession. Fireworks that had been strung along the trolley tracks were lit as la Madonna approached, making a carpet of noise and smoke for her....Pushcart vendors saluted as the Madonna was carried past the great outdoor Italian market on First Avenue. Women and girls shouted entreaties over the heads of the crowd to their patroness....Others pushed their way through the crowd, or pushed their children through the crowd, to pin money onto the banner. In front of the image was a small box into which people threw money and jewelry....

At the very rear of the procession walked the penitents. All of them walked barefoot; some crawled along on their hands and knees....Some of the women in the rear had disheveled hair and bloodied faces, and women of all ages walked with their hair undone. Some people wore special robes—white robes with a blue sash like Mary's or Franciscan-style brown robes knotted at the waist with a cord....

When the tour of Italian Harlem was over, the procession returned to the doors of the church, where la Madonna was greeted with a round of fireworks and, in the earlier days, gunshot. Then the people lined up to wait for hours for their turn to enter the sanctuary and present their petitions....

The pilgrims had only a moment at the altar because others were pushing up behind them. From the priests on the altar they received a scapular, which they valued as protection from all harm. They paused for a brief moment to say a prayer to la Madonna, and then they made their way back outside. The line waiting in the July night stretched down 115th Street to First Avenue, where it went along for blocks.... Men and women who grew up in East Harlem but left it in the 1940s and 1950s still remember the feast day of Our Lady of Mount Carmel as a very special time, a time of gaiety and parties that lasted for a week, but also a time of serious religious dedication.

A badge from the 1911 ceremony dedicating a statue of Christopher Columbus in Walla Walla, Washington.

At the Festa dei Gigli (Feast of the Lilies), Italian Americans carry a large tower (called the giglio, *or "lily") through the streets of Queens, New York. The celebration, which also takes place in other U.S. cities, originated in the town of Nola, Italy. It honors Saint Paolino, a 5th-century bishop who rescued prisoners from the invading Vandals. The citizens of Nola greeted Bishop Paolino with lilies; over the centuries the flowers "grew" into these elaborate towers.*

117

Theresa F. Bucchieri (the child ar right), with her family around 1914. From left are her grandmother "Nonna" Serafina Passalacqua, father Antonio Bucchieri, and mother Giuseppina. Theresa's brother John is the child on the left.

THE BUCCHIERI FAMILY

South Philadelphia is a community of families. Here, 25 blocks south of Independence Hall, where the Declaration of Independence was signed, Italian immigrants built their neighborhood in the late 19th century: South Philly.

When Theresa F. Bucchieri comes to the door of her house, she looks amazingly young for her 84 years. Inside, the walls are covered with mementoes, photographs of friends and family, and paintings. Bucchieri, who began her career as a journalist, starts the interview herself.

Theresa Bucchieri:

All these paintings were done by people I have known, many of whom have passed on to their eternal reward. See, they are precious memories. That beautiful painting of an autumn scene of the Cumberland Valley was presented to me by the people of Chambersburg, Pennsylvania, where I worked as an employee of the U.S. Department of Labor. Everything in this house has a memory. Here is a large, beautiful painting of the town of Taormina, Sicily. I got it when I visited my cousins there.

Q: Did your parents ever say why they decided to emigrate?

Oh, yes, sure. They said, *La Miseria*—too much misery. We went to America to prosper. My father arrived in 1904. He was engaged to my mother Giuseppina Passalacqua at the time, but she stayed in Sicily. He called for her after a year. She lived with a relative until they got married.

I was born in 1908. My brother John came along in 1910 and my sister Sara arrived in 1917. My parents opened up a mom-and-pop grocery store. Above it was our big, ten-room house. It was an integrated neighborhood, and we had all different kinds of people as customers. Next door lived a lovely couple–she was Puerto Rican and he was black. We also had Jewish and Irish. When I went to college and met different kinds of people, I felt perfectly at home.

Q: It was unusual for women to go to college in those days, wasn't it?

It was quite a rare thing to send your daughter even to high school. I would say my mother was avant-garde in this way: she insisted that her daughters go to college. Not all parents were like mine. Due to circumstances, their children had to work or attend trade school. My mother's friends said, "You're going to send your daughter to college? Why, she'll get married soon and her education will go down the drain."

My mother said, "No, no, she'll get married when she finds somebody as good as she is." And then they had to keep quiet. I'll never forget, my mother said, "No, my daughter's going to go to college." I went to Temple University, here in Philadelphia, majored in journalism.

Q: Your sister went there too?

My sister went to the Philadelphia School of Industrial Art. She went into the commercial art field until she married. Her husband's name is Leo Campanella. Here's a picture of their family. I call it the royal family.

My brother John did not want to go to college. John got a job with Food Fair [a supermarket chain] and eventually became manager of the grocery department.

My nieces and nephews are all happily married to non-Italians. We have a Pole, a Swiss, a Scot, a German, Irish, English. So we're the League of Nations. And that's great, it's great.

Q: When you were growing up, did you carry on any special Italian traditions?

Oh yes. When my mother came here, she left her mother and sister behind in Sicily. And then a few years later, my father, God bless him, sent for his mother-in-law, who we called Nonna, or grandmum, Serafina. She was 75 when we took that picture [a large tinted photo in an oval frame over the mantel]. And then he sent for my Aunt Antonia, my mother's sister.

We always celebrated St. Joseph's Feast Day, March 19, because it was my mother's Name Day–Giuseppina. Every St. Joseph Day we'd bake the traditional *crispeddi*–a light, flaky doughnut stuffed with raisins and ricotta cheese. We always celebrated the 13th of June, St. Anthony's Day, because it was my father's Name Day plus my parents' wedding anniversary.

And of course at Christmastime, we had a very traditional holiday with a Christmas tree and an imported Sicilian manger. I have a memory from when I was a little girl. I was dressed as a priest, carrying the statue of Baby Jesus down from the attic to the living room. There, the older relatives were playing Italian Christmas songs on the Victrola.

All my little cousins were following me in procession when I slipped and fell down the attic steps and they all fell on top of me. My uncle, my father, my mother, everybody came up to see what happened. All they could see was a lot of legs and arms. Here I was underneath a pile of children, holding tight to the statue, and would you believe the Baby Jesus emerged unscathed?

Q: It's not unusual for women to have careers today, but it was when you graduated from college.

Antonio Bucchieri is shown in the family's grocery store in South Philadelphia around 1922 in this old and damaged photograph. "Everybody called him Tony," wrote his daughter Theresa in one of her books

This framed photograph of Nonna Serafina hangs over the mantel in Theresa Bucchieri's home today.

Eleanor Morton

Tells of Contributions Made by Italian-Americans, Bringing Traditions of an Old Country to a New Land

THE other evening the Circolo Dante Alighieri held the initiation ceremonies of a new women's group, a club of American girls of Italian extraction, meeting to introduce new members and to present their charter to the organization.

There was a quite charming stateliness in the meeting and program—a reminiscence of old Roman days, which perhaps modern girls of another background would not have the unself-consciousness to present and to enjoy as well. The young woman at the president's table sat before two lighted candles; beside her were two officers; on the tiny platform sat another young lady waiting to play the piano. She struck her first note as the initiates began to come in, and slowly, very solemnly, the young members began to march in, two by two, their evening costumes making a curious and most beguiling adornment to faces of many varying Italian types, but all types represented by very pretty girls. Behind them sat beaming parents and swains.

THE girls made a number of speeches. There was the usual youthful display of fireworks of phraseology, the usual ardent piling up of figures of speech. It was like the commencement in some high school or college. And, as in high school or college, the speakers discussed great issues, affairs of the world and of its future.

But there was one difference of peculiar interest in this meeting. The speakers stressed, with conscious appreciation, and with a very high sincerity, the debt they owe to help make great the issues which will be met by their generation, and they spoke, intelligently and yet with stirring ardor, of the debt they owe from which they were building their life, the American which is their present, the Italian which is their past.

One appreciates the concrete proof of their feeling along these directions. Of the two speeches made, the first was in English, and its theme was "What Is Americanism?" the second was in Italian, and its subject was "The Contribution of Italians to the Culture of the World." Both speakers were young Philadelphia teachers. They were, therefore, speaking not only for their cultural attainments, but for the contribution they—as Italian-American women—are making to the whole American life today.

BUT perhaps most appealing was the recognition they expressed of the debt they, inheritors of a new land its opportunity, owe to their parents.

A young speaker spoke of that, and one wanted to applaud.

"We cannot forget that our parents made great sacrifices for us, to enable us to have an education," she said, and the applause came instantly. That is the best of these young people; it bespeaks the quality and the vision that they are planning to make the spirit of their new club, called, appropriately, "L'Aurora Society."

Will Preside

THERESA F. BUCCHIERI
Founder of L'Aurora Society, who will be mistress of ceremonies at the club's formal initiation exercises to be held tomorrow night at Circolo Dante Alighiere

A 1930s newspaper clipping describes the formation of L'Aurora Society for young Italian American women. Theresa F. Bucchieri, shown in the photograph, was the mistress of ceremonies at the inaugural of the group.

Theresa Bucchieri calls this her "prize possession"—the certificate that the Department of Labor awarded to her on her retirement after 30 years of service.

The United States Department of Labor

CERTIFICATE OF SERVICE

Theresa F. Bucchieri

Upon the occasion of your retirement this Certificate is presented in recognition of

Thirty years

of honorable service to the Government of the United States

When I graduated from Temple University in 1931 I became a newspaper writer. I think I must have been the first Italian American journalist in this area. I wrote for the *Public Ledger*. Due to my knowledge of the Italian language, I was assigned to interview Italian dignitaries visiting the United States, such as Dino Grande, Italy's foreign minister; and the inventor Guglielmo Marconi. Dino Grande sent me a beautiful telegram saying how wonderful it was to meet an Italian American woman journalist.

Another exciting experience was when the newspaper's music critic asked me, "How would you like to go to New York and interview the Metropolitan Opera stars?" I said, "I'd love it!" I was there two weeks, and I sat in the box of the manager of the Opera Company. I interviewed Ezio Pinza, Giovanni Martinelli, Benjamin Gigli, Lily Pons, Rosa Ponselle, and a few others.

Then, after the *Public Ledger* went out of business, I took a civil-service examination in 1938. At that time Congress had enacted the Fair Labor Standards Act, which set a minimum wage for workers. I was appointed to the U.S. Department of Labor's Wage and Hour Division, which was in charge of administering and enforcing the Act. I worked there 30 years.

I started as an investigator, and incidentally I was the first woman of Italian extraction in the Wage and Hour Division. When the time came for a promotion, I was appointed supervising investigator. The only woman supervisor. I had 18 investigators under my supervision. Nine were men, and they didn't like the idea of having a lady boss. So they tried to make it a little hard for me.

So I said to those men under my supervision, "You're not working for me. We're working together as a team. We're working for Uncle Sam." That kind of appeased them. I got myself into their good graces this way: When one of them would make a mistake, I'd say, "How did *we* miss the boat?" I always involved myself, though I had nothing to do with the mistake. And when they would do excellent work—with my help—I'd say, "Gee, John, you did a terrific job. You're terrific." And that really slayed them. They're still my friends.

Q: You wrote books, too.

I'll never forget when my first book was published, *Feasting with Nonna Serafina*. It's not just a cookbook, it's a collection of memories of all the great times we had feasting on Nonna Serafina's cooking in every month of the year. It was sold all over the country. When I went to London, I saw my book on sale in Harrod's Department Store. That was great!

I was to accompany my father on a visit to Sicily in 1936, but he died suddenly. A year later I went alone and wrote my *Journal of Sicilian Reminiscences*. When I returned, I lived in the big house over the grocery store with my mother, my grandmother, my brother and sister. Eventually they married, and I was left with my mother and grandmother.

In the meantime, my Aunt Antonia's husband died and she now lived alone in her little house. My mother invited her to live with us. She readily accepted, rented her house, and moved in with us, which turned out to be lucky. My precious grandmother died in 1947 at age 94. Then my mother had a stroke in 1950. I was working for the Labor Department then, and I was fortunate that my aunt was there to help me.

My mother died in 1952. So that left just me and my aunt, and I said, "What are we going to do in this big house? We're *due moschi*—two flies—in this big house." So she said, "Come live with me in my little house."

So I've been living here since 1953. Now in 1968, my aunt got sick. She had what they call Alzheimer's today, and I had to take early retirement from the Labor Department to be with her. I took care of her until 1977, when she died. As a result, I wrote another book, *Keep Your Old Folks at Home.* I wanted to show people that they didn't have to put their elderly relatives into nursing homes. I received a lot of letters about this book, some from Congressmen and Senators, and the book helped in a little way to bring about better health-care laws.

Q: During your career, did you ever experience any discrimination because you were an Italian American?

Not at work...socially yes! When I told some people I lived in South Philadelphia, they said, "Oh! Mafia Town!" It saddened and distressed me when unintelligent people associated all Sicilians with the Mafia. I emphasized that only 2 percent of Sicilians are Mafiosi and 98 percent are good and special people. My role model was my father, who was a prince, and my brother, another prince!

Q: Do you have any advice for young people today?

My motto is "Follow your dream." People ask me, "You have any problems, Theresa?" Of course I've had my share, but I look upon problems as challenges. I inherited that spirit from my parents who came to America—a new land, with a language barrier, inferior housing, no employment waiting for them. Imagine what courage it took for them to come to America. And yet they survived.

All this adjustment entailed hard work, faith and hope. God bless that courageous generation. A lot of young people don't appreciate what wonderful ancestors they had. I'm writing my memoirs, just for my nieces and nephews. I am very proud of my heritage and I want them to be proud of their roots. I have 9 great-nieces and nephews, and 9 great-great-nieces and nephews.

I have a little poem for them:
Yesterday is a memory
Tomorrow is a dream
All you have is the magic of today
Make the best of it
And to God you leave the rest.

The covers of three books by Bucchieri. Each was inspired by parts of her family's history, both in Italy and the United States.

Theresa Bucchieri (standing at right) with her sister's family. From left, back row, are Terry Campanella Moore, Alissa Sara Moore, Alan W. Moore, Jr., and Leo A. Campanella. Seated are Leo L. Campanella, Alan W. Moore III, and Sara Bucchieri Campanella.

The three children of Antonio and Giuseppina Bucchieri: Sara (born 1917), John (born 1910), and Theresa (born 1908).

ITALIAN AMERICAN TIMELINE

1492
Cristoforo Colombo makes his first voyage to America.

1498
Giovanni Caboto sails down the northeast coast of America to Chesapeake Bay.

1502
Returning from a trip to America, Amerigo Vespucci declares that the land is not part of Asia, but "a New World."

1524
Giovanni da Verrazano sails into New York Harbor and follows the coast south to Florida.

1539
Marco da Nizza journeys north from Mexico into present-day Arizona.

1681-1711
Father Eusebio Chino establishes missions in lower California and Arizona.

1682
Enrico Tonti accompanies La Salle down the Mississippi River to the Gulf of Mexico.1773

1773
Filippo Mazzei arrives in Virginia, later joins Patriot cause in the American Revolution.

1779
Francisco Vigo supplies information that helps George Rogers Clark defeat the British at Vincennes, Indiana.

1849
Discovery of gold in California lures Italians to San Francisco area.

1855
Castle Garden in New York is opened as a landing station for immigrants.

1855
Constantino Brumidi is hired to paint frescoes in the Capitol in Washington, D.C.; he continues the work until his death in 1880.

1860
Giuseppe Garibaldi leads his Redshirts into Sicily.

1861
Italy becomes a kingdom, with capital at Turin.

1871-1920
More than 4 million Italians immigrate to the United States.

1880
First daily Italian American newspaper, *Il Progresso Italo-Americano*, begins publication in New York City.

1889
Francesca Cabrini arrives in America to begin work among Italian immigrants.

1891
Eleven Sicilian immigrants are lynched in New Orleans.

1892
Ellis Island immigration station opens in New York.

1904
A. P. Giannini founds Bank of Italy in San Francisco.

1905
Sons of Italy founded by Dr. Vincenzo Sellaro.

1921
Congress passes a law limiting new immigration, instituting a quota system based on the census of 1910.

1924
Congress passes the National Origins Act, which reduces new immigration to 2 percent of the total of each foreign nation's population in the United States in the census of 1890. After this time, Italian immigration dropped sharply.

1933
Fiorello La Guardia elected mayor of New York.

1941
United States enters World War II against Japan, Germany, and Italy.

1944
Passage of G.I. Bill of Rights, which provided low-cost loans and college tuition for veterans of World War II.

1946
John Pastore elected governor of Rhode Island.

1965
New immigration law phases out national-origins formula.

1969
Salvatore Luria receives the Nobel Prize for medicine.

1984
Geraldine Ferraro nominated for Vice President of the United States.

FURTHER READING

General Accounts of Italian American History

DiStasi, Lawrence, ed. *Dream Streets: The Big Book of Italian-American Culture*. New York: Harper & Row, 1989.

Gallo, Patrick J. *Old Bread, New Wine: A Portrait of the Italian-Americans*. Chicago: Nelson-Hall, 1981.

Gambino, Richard. *Blood of My Blood*. Garden City, N.Y.: Doubleday, 1974.

Iorizzo, Luciano J., and Salvatore Modello. *The Italian Americans*. Boston: Twayne, 1980.

Mangione, Jerre, and Ben Morreale. *La Storia*. New York: Harper-Collins, 1992.

Musmanno, Michael A. *The Story of the Italians in America*. Garden City, N.Y.: Doubleday, 1965.

Nelli, Humbert S. *From Immigrants to Ethnics*. New York: Oxford University Press, 1983.

Rolle, Andrew. *The Italian Americans*. New York: Free Press, 1980.

Schiavo, Giovanni. *Four Centuries of Italian-American History*. New York: Vigo Press, 1958.

Schoener, Allon. *The Italian Americans*. New York: Macmillan, 1987.

Personal Accounts of Italian American Life

Bucchieri, Theresa F. *Feasting with Nonna Serafina: A Guide to the Italian Kitchen*. Cranbury, N.J.: A. S. Barnes, 1966.

Canevali, Emanuel. *Autobiography*. New York: Horizon, 1967.

Cateura, Linda Brandi. *Growing Up Italian*. New York: William Morrow, 1987.

Cohen, David Steven, ed. *America, the Dream of My Life*. New Brunswick, N.J.: Rutgers University Press, 1990.

D'Angelo, Pascal. *Son of Italy*. 1924. Reprint. New York: Arno Press, 1975.

Ewen, Elizabeth. *Immigrant Women in the Land of Dollars*. New York: Monthly Review Press, 1985.

Gisolfi, Anthony M. *Caudine Country: The Old World and an American Childhood*. New York: Senda Nueva de Ediciones, 1985.

Kessner, Thomas, and Betty Boyd Caroli. *Today's Immigrants: Their Stories*. New York: Oxford University Press, 1982.

Krause, Corinne Azen. *Grandmothers, Mothers, and Daughters*. Boston: Twayne, 1991.

La Guardia, Fiorello H. *The Making of an Insurgent: An Autobiography 1882-1919*. 1948. Reprint. New York: Capricorn Books, 1961.

La Sorte, Michael. *La Merica: Images of Italian Greenhorn Experience*. Philadelphia: Temple University Press, 1985.

Leone, Gene. *Leone's Italian Cookbook*. New York: Harper & Row, 1967.

Maglione, Connie A., and Carmen Anthony Fiore. *Voices of the Daughters*. Princeton, N.J.: Townhouse, 1989.

Mangione, Jerre. *An Ethnic at Large*. Philadelphia: University of Pennsylvania Press, 1983.

Massalo, Arthur D., trans. *The Wonderful Life of Angelo Massari*. New York: Exposition Press, 1965.

Morrison, Joan, and Charlotte Fox Zabusky, eds. *American Mosaic*. New York: Dutton, 1980.

Pellegrini, Angelo. *American Dream: An Immigrant's Quest*. San Francisco: North Point Press, 1986.

Pellegrini, Angelo. *Immigrant's Return*. New York: Macmillan, 1952.

Santoli, Al. *The New Americans: An Oral History*. New York: Viking, 1988.

Talese, Gay. *Unto the Sons*. New York: Knopf, 1992.

Novels of Italian American Life

D'Agostino, Guido. *Olives on the Apple Tree*. New York: Doubleday, Doran, 1940.

D'Ambrosio, Richard. *No Language But a Cry*. Garden City, N.Y.: Doubleday, 1970.

De Capite, Michael. *Maria*. New York: John Day, 1943.

Di Donato, Pietro. *Christ in Concrete*. Indianapolis: Bobbs-Merrill, 1939.

Fante, John. *Brotherhood of the Grape*. Boston: Houghton Mifflin, 1977.

Forgione, Louis. *The River Between*. New York: Arno Press, 1975.

Puzo, Mario. *The Fortunate Pilgrim*. New York: Atheneum, 1964.

TEXT CREDITS

Main Text

p. 12, top: Corinne Azen Krause, *Grandmothers, Mothers, and Daughters* (Boston: Twayne, 1991), 51.

p. 12, bottom: Pascal D'Angelo, *Son of Italy* (1924; reprint, New York: Arno Press, 1975), 2.

p. 13: Reprinted with the permission of Macmillan Publishing Company from *Immigrant's Return* by Angelo M. Pellegrini. Copyright 1951, renewed 1979 by Angelo M. Pellegrini. Pp. 11-20.

p. 15: Michael La Sorte, *La Merica: Images of Italian Greenhorn Experience* (Philadelphia: Temple University Press, 1985), 107.

p. 16, top: Arthur D. Massalo, trans., *The Wonderful Life of Angelo Massari* (New York: Exposition Press, 1965), 46-47.

p. 16, bottom: D'Angelo, *Son of Italy*, 47-48.

p. 17, top: La Sorte, *La Merica*, 33-34.

p. 17, middle: Stefano Miele, "America as a Place to Make Money," *World's Work* 41 (December 1920): 204.

p. 17, bottom: Ivan Chermayeff, et al., *Ellis Island: An Illustrated History of the Immigrant Experience* (New York: Macmillan, 1991), 25-26.

p. 20: Richard Hakluyt, *The Voyages...and Discoveries of Foreign Voyagers*, vol. 10 (1600; reprint, London: J. M. Dent, 1928), 157-59.

p. 21: Giovanni Schiavo, *The Italians in America Before the Civil War* (1934; reprint, New York: Arno Press, 1975), 109.

p. 22, top: Reprinted with the permission of Macmillan Publishing Company from *Immigrant's Return* by Angelo M. Pellegrini. Copyright 1951, renewed 1979 by Angelo M. Pellegrini. Pp. 29-30.

p. 22, bottom: Massalo, *The Wonderful Life of Angelo Massari*, 77-79.

p. 23: David A. Taylor and John Alexander Williams, eds., *Old Ties, New Attachments: Italian-American Folklife in the West* (Washington, D.C.: Library of Congress, 1992), 82-83.

p. 24, top: Jerre Mangione and Ben Morreale, *La Storia* (New York: Harper/Collins, 1992), 101.

p. 24, bottom: Massalo, *The Wonderful Life of Angelo Massari*, 79-80.

p. 25: Michael A. La Sorte, trans., "Diary of Totonno Pappatore," *Attenzione!* (Jan. 1981): 31-32.

p. 26: Edmondo De Amicis, *On Blue Water*, trans. Jacob B. Brown (New York: Putnam, 1907), 1-11.

p. 27: Nathan Glazer and Daniel P. Moynihan, *Beyond the Melting Pot* (Cambridge: MIT Press, 1970), 30-32.

p. 28, top: Willard Heaps, *The Story of Ellis Island* (New York: Seabury Press, 1967), 41-42.

p. 28, bottom: Francesco Ventresca, *Personal Reminiscences of a Naturalized American* (New York: Rueson, 1937), 20.

p. 29, top: La Sorte, *La Merica*, 25.

p. 30, bottom: Hamilton Holt, ed., *Life Stories of Undistinguished Americans* (1906; reprint, New York: Routledge, 1990), 33.

p. 34: Richard J. Gulick, et al., *Italy and the Italians in Washington's Time* (New York: Arno Press, 1975), 106-7.

p. 35, top: Philip Di Franco, *The Italian American Experience* (New York: Tor Books, 1988), 41.

p. 35, bottom: Myrtle Cheney Murdock, *Constantino Brumidi* (Washington, D.C.: Monumental Press, 1950), 6, 71.

p. 36, La Sorte, *La Merica*, 52-54.

p. 37: La Sorte, *La Merica*, 41-42.

p. 38: Mangione and Morreale, *La Storia*, 113.

p. 39: Reprinted with the permission of Macmillan Publishing Company from *Immigrant's Return* by Angelo M. Pellegrini. Copyright 1951, renewed 1979 by Angelo M. Pellegrini. Pp. 32-36.

p. 40, top: Taylor and Williams, *Old Ties, New Attachments*, 82-83.

p. 40, bottom: D'Angelo, *Son of Italy*, 59-61.

p. 41: Wayne Moquin and Charles Van Doren, *A Documentary History of the Italian Americans* (New York: Praeger, 1974), 389-390.

p. 46: Holt, *Life Stories*, 34-36.

p. 48, top: Erik Amfitheatrof, *The Children of Columbus* (Boston: Little Brown, 1973), 162-63.

p. 48, bottom: Francesco Cordasco and Eugene Buccioni, *The Italians: Social Backgrounds of an American Group* (Clifton, N.J.: Augustus Kelly Publications, 1974), 393-94.

p. 49: David Steven Cohen, ed., *America the Dream of My Life* (New Brunswick, N.J.: Rutgers University Press, 1990), 65-66.

p. 50: Constantine Panunzio, *The Soul of an Immigrant* (New York: Macmillan, 1937), 75-77.

p. 51: Massalo, *The Wonderful Life of Angelo Massari*, 91-92.

p. 52: Moquin and Van Doren, *Documentary History*, 82-83.

p. 53, top: Luciano J. Iorizzo and Salvatore Mondello, *The Italian-Americans* (Boston: Twayne, 1971), 116.

p. 53, bottom: Giles R. Wright and Howard L. Green, *Work*, New Jersey Ethnic Life Series (Trenton, N.J.: New Jersey Historical Commission, 1987), 17-18.

p. 54: Reprinted from *American Mosaic: The Immigrant Experience in the Words of Those Who Lived It*, by Joan Morrison and Charlotte Fox Zabusky, by permission of the University of Pittsburgh Press. © 1980, 1993 by Joan Morrison and Charlotte Fox Zabusky, 63-64.

p. 55, top: Chermayeff, *Ellis Island*, 65.

p. 55, bottom: Chermayeff, *Ellis Island*, 67.

p. 56, top: Elizabeth Ewen, *Immigrant Women in the Land of Dollars* (New York: Monthly Review Press, 1985), 244. Copyright © 1985 by Elizabeth Ewen. Reprinted by permission of Monthly Review Foundation.

p. 56, second from top: Ewen, *Immigrant Women*, 246-247. Copyright © 1985 by Elizabeth Ewen. Reprinted by permission of Monthly Review Foundation.

p. 56, third from top: Ewen, *Immigrant Women*, 247. Copyright © 1985 by Elizabeth Ewen. Reprinted by permission of Monthly Review Foundation.

p. 56, bottom: Ewen, *Immigrant Women*, 251. Copyright © 1985 by Elizabeth Ewen. Reprinted by permission of Monthly Review Foundation.

p. 58: Amfitheatrof, *Children of Columbus*, 181-82.

p. 60, top: Moquin and Van Doren, *Documentary History*, 366-68.

p. 60, bottom: Francesco Cordasco, ed., *Studies in Italian American Social History* (Totowa, N.J.: Rowman and Littlefield, 1975), 207.

p. 61, top: Fiorello H. La Guardia, *The Making of an Insurgent* (1948; reprint, New York: Capricorn Books, 1961), 27.

p. 61, bottom: Mangione and Morreale, *La Storia*, 299-300.

p. 62: Moquin and Van Doren, *Documentary History*, 64-65.

p. 68: Alice Lynd and Staughton Lynd, eds., *Rank and File: Personal Histories by Working-Class Organizers* (Boston: Beacon Press, 1973), 134-36.

p. 70: Allon Schoener, *The Italian Americans* (New York: Macmillan, 1987), 207-9.

p. 71, top: Joseph Giordano, ed., *The Italian-American Catalog* (Garden City, N.Y.: Doubleday, 1986), 221-22.

p. 71, bottom: Richard Gambino, *Blood of My Blood* (Garden City, N.Y.: Doubleday, 1974), 167.

p. 72, top: Cordasco, *Studies*, 201.

p. 72, bottom: Mangione and Morreale, *La Storia*, 145.

p. 73, top: Panunzio, *The Soul of an Immigrant*, 228.

p. 73, bottom: Mangione and Morreale, *La Storia*, 167-68.

p. 74, top: Mangione and Morreale, *La Storia*, 145.

p. 74, bottom: Mangione and Morreale, *La Storia*, 137.

p. 75: Moquin and Van Doren, *Documentary History*, 47-48.

p. 76: Krause, *Grandmothers, Mothers, and Daughters*, 24-25.

p. 77: Cordasco, *Studies*, 434-48.

p. 78: Mangione and Morreale, *La Storia*, 225.

p. 79: Schoener, *The Italian Americans*, 207.

p. 80, top: Humbert S. Nelli, *From Immigrants to Ethnics* (New York: Oxford, 1983), 144.

p. 80, middle: Ewen, *Immigrant Women*, 200. Copyright © 1985 by Elizabeth Ewen. Reprinted by permission of Monthly Review Foundation.

p. 80, bottom: Ewen, *Immigrant Women*, 202. Copyright © 1985 by Elizabeth Ewen. Reprinted by permission of Monthly Review Foundation.

p. 81, top: Ewen, *Immigrant Women*, 236. Copyright © 1985 by Elizabeth Ewen. Reprinted by permission of Monthly Review Foundation.

p. 81, bottom: Andrew Rolle, *The Italian Americans* (New York: Free Press, 1980), 33.

p. 82: Anthony M. Gisolfi, *Caudine Country: The Old World and an American Childhood* (New York: Senda Nueva de Ediciones, 1985), 193-97.

p. 84: Mangione and Morreale, *La Storia*, 333.

p. 85, top: Ewen, *Immigrant Women*, 141. Copyright © 1985 by Elizabeth Ewen. Reprinted by permission of Monthly Review Foundation.

p. 85, bottom: Cordasco, *Studies*, 47.

p. 86, top: Reprinted with the permission of Macmillan Publishing Company from *Immigrant's Return* by Angelo M. Pellegrini. Copyright 1951, renewed 1979 by Angelo M. Pellegrini. P. 44.

p. 86, bottom: Panunzio, *Soul of An Immigrant*, 164-65.

p. 87, top: Panunzio, *Soul of An Immigrant*, 254-55.

p. 87, bottom: Connie A. Maglione and Carmen Anthony Fiore, *Voices of the Daughters* (Princeton, N.J.: Townhouse Publishing, 1989) 65-66.

p. 88: Moquin and Van Doren, *Documentary History*, 329-30.

p. 89, top: Cordasco, *Studies*, 209.

p. 89, bottom: Mangione and Morreale, *La Storia*, 142.

p. 90, top: Patrick J. Gallo, *Old Bread, New Wine* (Chicago: Nelson-Hall, 1981), 12.

p. 90, bottom: George R. Gilkey, ed., *Italian Emigrant Letters*, typescript from Wisconsin State University in archives of Center for Migration Studies, Staten Island, New York.

p. 91, top: Panunzio, *Soul of an Immigrant*, 324-25.

p. 91, middle: Mangione and Morreale, *La Storia*, 23.

p. 91, bottom: Moquin and Van Doren, *Documentary History*, 379-384.

p. 92: Gay Talese, *Unto the Sons* (New York: Ballantine, 1993), 583, 612-13.

p. 98: Krause, *Grandmothers, Mothers, and Daughters,* 19-22.

p. 99: Krause, *Grandmothers, Mothers, and Daughters,* 30-31.

p. 100, top: Krause, *Grandmothers, Mothers, and Daughters,* 31-32.

p. 100, bottom: Krause, *Grandmothers, Mothers, and Daughters,* 33-46.

p. 102, top: Maglione and Fiore, *Voices of the Daughters,* 31-32.

p. 102, bottom: Maglione and Fiore, *Voices of the Daughters,* 89.

p. 103: Linda Brandi Cateura, *Growing Up Italian* (New York: William Morrow, 1989), 235-37.

p. 104: Joseph Giordano, "Families," *Attenzione!* (Jan. 1980): 98-99.

p. 105: Cateura, *Growing Up Italian,* 245-48.

p. 106: Cateura, *Growing Up Italian,* 94-95.

p. 107: "The Apollo," from *New Americans: An Oral History* by Al Santoli. Copyright © 1988 by Al Santoli. Used by permission of Viking Penguin, a division of Penguin books USA Inc., 301-5.

p. 110: Theresa F. Bucchieri, *Feasting with Nonna Serafina: A Guide to the Italian Kitchen* (Cranbury, N.J.: A. S. Barnes, 1966), 7-10.

p. 111: Gene Leone, *Leone's Italian Cookbook* (New York: Harper & Row, 1967), 1-4.

p. 114, top: Mangione and Morreale, *La Storia,* 170-71.

p. 114, bottom: Robert A. Orsi, *The Madonna of 115th Street* (New Haven: Yale University Press, 1985), 1-12. © 1985 by Robert A. Orsi.

Sidebars

p. 13: Jerre Mangione and Ben Morreale, *La Storia* (New York: Harper/Collins, 1992), 81.

p. 14: Humbert S. Nelli, *From Immigrants to Ethnics: The Italian Americans* (New York: Oxford, 1983), 28, 135, 146.

p. 17: Andrew Rolle, *The Immigrant Upraised: Italian Adventurers and Colonists in an Expanding America* (Norman: University of Oklahoma Press, 1971), 25.

p. 22: Allon Schoener, *The Italian Americans* (New York: Macmillan, 1987), 56-57.

p. 23: David A. Taylor and John Alexander Williams, eds., *Old Ties, New Attachments: Italian-American Folklife in the West* (Washington, D.C.: Library of Congress, 1992), 82-83.

p. 24: Michael La Sorte, *La Merica: Images of Italian Greenhorn Experience* (Philadelphia: Temple University Press, 1985), 13.

p. 26: From *The Ellis Island Immigrant Cookbook* by Tom Bernardin, copyright 1991 Tom Bernardin, NYC, NY, 125.

p. 28: La Sorte, *La Merica,* 202.

p. 35: Wayne Moquin and Charles Van Doren, eds., *A Documentary History of the Italian Americans* (New York: Praeger, 1974), 32.

p. 38: Ivan Chermayeff, et al., *Ellis Island: An Illustrated History of the Immigrant Experience* (New York: Macmillan, 1991), 154.

p. 39: Chermayeff, *Ellis Island,* 134.

p. 40: Mangione and Morreale, *La Storia,* 125.

p. 41: Mangione and Morreale, *La Storia,* 109.

p. 47: Mangione and Morreale, *La Storia,* 163.

p. 48: Pascal D'Angelo, *Son of Italy,* (1924; reprint, New York: Arno Press), 180-81.

p. 55: Mangione and Morreale, *La Storia,* 133-34.

p. 56: Elizabeth Ewen, *Immigrant Women in the Land of Dollars* (New York: Monthly Review Press, 1985), 173. Copyright © 1985 by Elizabeth Ewen. Reprinted by permission of Monthly Review Foundation.

p. 58: Ewen, *Immigrant Women,* 258. Copyright © 1985 by Elizabeth Ewen. Reprinted by permission of Monthly Review Foundation.

p. 59: Mangione and Morreale, *La Storia,* 293.

p. 60: Patrick J. Gallo, *Old Bread, New Wine* (Chicago: Nelson-Hall, 1981), 116.

p. 62: Lawrence DiStasi, ed., *Dream Streets* (New York: Harper & Row, 1989), 14, 16.

p. 69: Moquin and Van Doren, *A Documentary History,* 314-15.

p. 70: Mangione and Morrele, *La Storia,* 160.

p. 76, top: Rolle, *The Immigrant Upraised,* 11.

p. 76, bottom: Gladys Nadler Rips, *Coming to America: Immigrants from Southern Europe* (New York: Delacorte Press, 1983), 44.

p. 77: Chermayeff, *Ellis Island,* 75.

p. 78: Luigi Barzini, *The Italians* (New York: Harper & Row, 1964), 198.

p. 83: Anthony M. Gisolfi, *Caudine Country* (New York: Senda Nueva de Ediciones, 1985), 195-196.

p. 87: Mangione and Morreale, *La Storia,* 226.

p. 88: Nelli, *From Immigrants to Ethnics,* 98.

p. 90: Andrew Rolle, *The Italian Americans: Troubled Roots* (New York: Free Press, 1980), 55.

p. 111: Theresa F. Bucchieri, *Feasting with Nonna Serafina: A Guide to the Italian Kitchen* (Cranbury, N.J.: A. S. Barnes, 1966), 21-22.

p. 116: Rolle, *The Immigrant Upraised,* 302-3.

p. 117: DiStasi, *Dream Streets,* 240.

PICTURE CREDITS

Aldrich Public Library, Barre, Vt.: 8, 40; Alice Austen, Staten Island Historical Society Collection: 54 bottom, 73, 74; Balch Institute for Ethnic Studies Library: frontispiece (Joseph Fidanza photographs), 11 (Belfiore family photographs), 23 (Balch Reproductions), 44 (Carmen Giorgio photograph), 47 (Crystal Water Company photographs), 68 and 89 top (Leonard Covello photographs), 82 (DiMarco family photographs), 97 (Rosemarie Corto photographs), 96 (Carolfi photographs), 98 middle and bottom (Justave family photographs), 116 (Our Lady of Mount Carmel Photographs), 119 top (Bucchieri family photographs); Bank of America Archives: 63 top; Bostonian Society/Old State House: 75 bottom; Brown Brothers: 27, 58 bottom; California Historical Society, San Francisco: 62 (Photographers: Turrill and Miller, FN-21959); Carpenter Center for Visual Arts, Harvard University: 13, 57 top; Center for Migration Studies, Staten Island, N.Y.: 18, 25, 28, 41 top, 42, 53, 60, 61 top, 117 bottom; © Martha Cooper, City Lore: 94; Festa Italiana (The Italian Community Center) Milwaukee, Wis.: cover, 23 top, 64, 76, 77, 79, 86; courtesy Greater Boston Convention and Visitors' Bureau, 104 bottom; Ellen Hoobler: 114, 115 bottom; Collection of Immigrant City Archives, Lawrence, Mass.: 58 top; Institute of Texan Cultures, San Antonio, Tex.: 12, 15, 21, 33, 63 bottom, 89 bottom; Italian American Collection, Special Collections, The University Library, The University of Illinois at Chicago: 81 bottom, 84 bottom; Labor-Management Documentation Center, Cornell University: 56, 59; Library of Congress: 5, 10, 14, 17, 29 top, 35 bottom, 49 bottom, 52 bottom, 66, 67, 71 both, 72 top, 75 top, 80 top, 86 top, 87, 90, 92 both, 99, 104 top, 108 bottom, 109 bottom, 110, 111, 112, 113, 115 top, 117 top; Museum of the City of New York, Jacob A. Riis Collection: 69; National Archives: 32, 49 top, 54 top, 57 bottom, 82 bottom; National Park Service, Ellis Island Immigrant Museum: 38 bottom, 51, 81 top; National Park Service, Western Archeological and Conservation Center: 20, 21 top; Lewis W. Hine Collection, U.S. History, Local History & Genealogy Division, The New York Public Library, Astor, Lenox and Tilden Foundations: 18, 30, 38 top, 37 top, 50, 68 top, 72 bottom, 98 top; U.S. History, Local History & Genealogy Division, The New York Public Library, Astor, Lenox and Tilden Foundations: 37 bottom; New York Public Library for the Performing Arts, 35 top; Picture Collection, The Branch Libraries, The New York Public Library, 16; San Francisco Public Library: 45, 85; Eleanor Smeal, Feminist Majority Foundation: 101; Smithsonian Institution: 41 bottom; Edward A. Smyk, Passaic County (N.J.) Historian: 80 bottom; courtesy of the Statue of Liberty National Monument: 100; Supreme Court Historical Society: 108 top; UPI/Bettmann: 39, 61 bottom, 91, 106, 107, 109; Adam Clark Vroman, Courtesy Museum of New Mexico: 21 bottom; Washington County Historical Society, Fayetteville, Ark.: 52 top, 78; Western Reserve Historical Society: 46; Wide World Photos: 93 both, 105.

INDEX

ACKNOWLEDGMENTS

We owe a great debt of thanks to Mario Carini, historian of the Italian Community Center of Milwaukee, and to Diana Zimmerman of the Center for Migration Studies in Staten Island. This book would not have been possible without their generous contributions.

We also wish to express our gratitude to Patricia Akre of the San Francisco Library; Mary Ann Bamberger of the University of Illinois at Chicago; Tom Bernardin, author of *The Ellis Island Immigrant Cookbook*; Diane Bruce of the Institute of Texan Cultures at San Antonio; Janet Carter and Norma Torres, research consultants at the Bank of America; Ray Collins, Brown Brothers; Francesco Cordasco; Carlotta de Fillo of the Staten Island Historical Society; Tara Deal and Nancy Toff, our editors at Oxford University Press; Jeffrey Dosik of the National Park Service, Ellis Island Immigration Museum; Don Garate of the National Park Service at Tumacacori, Ariz.; Ronnie Hill of the Western Archeological Conservation Center in Tucson, Ariz.; Paul F. Iannelli, Executive Director of Festa Italiana; Thomas Jordan of the Washington County (Ark.) Historical Society; Jacquelyn M. Lucchese; Patricia Proscino Lusk and Jennifer Van Vlanderen of the Balch Institute for Ethnic Studies; Alice and Staughton Lynd; Connie A. Maglione and Carmen Anthony Fiore; Paulette Manos, New York State School of Industrial and Labor Relations, Cornell University; Lynn Marie Mitchell, Archivist, National Park Service, Western Archeological and Conservation Center; Barbara Norfleet and Elizabeth Kunreuther of the Carpenter Center for Visual Arts; Ann Sindelar and Michael McCormack of the Western Reserve Historical Society; Eleanor Smeal; Edward A. Smyk, Passaic County Historian, and Andrew Shick of the Passaic County (N.J.) Historical Society; Marjorie Strong of the Aldrich Public Library, Barre, Vt.; Gay Talese; and Jack Womack, Amalgamated Clothing and Textile Workers Union.

We owe special thanks to Theresa F. Bucchieri for her generosity in sharing her memories and her own Italian American family album. Theresa welcomed us to her home on a winter afternoon and told us the story of her life. We only wish that our book contained enough space for the entire interview. Theresa has been a dear friend and a source of inspiration throughout the writing of this book.

ABOUT THE AUTHORS

Dorothy and Thomas Hoobler have published more than 50 books for children and young adults, including *Italian Portraits; Margaret Mead: A Life in Science; Vietnam: Why We Fought; Showa: The Age of Hirohito;* and *Photographing History: The Career of Mathew Brady.* Their works have been honored by the Society for School Librarians International, the Library of Congress, the New York Public Library, the National Council for Social Studies, and *Best Books for Children,* among other organizations and publications. The Hooblers have also written several volumes of historical fiction for children, including *Frontier Diary, The Summer of Dreams,* and *Treasure in the Stream.* Dorothy Hoobler received her master's degree in American history from New York University and worked as a textbook editor before becoming a full-time freelance editor and writer. Thomas Hoobler received his master's degree in education from Xavier University and he previously worked as a teacher and textbook editor.